A Century of Films

Derek Malcolm's
Personal Best

A CENTURY OF FILMS

Derek Malcolm

TAURIS PARKE PAPERBACKS
LONDON • NEW YORK

Published in 2000 by I.B.Tauris & Co Ltd
Victoria House, Bloomsbury Square, London WC1B 4DZ
175 Fifth Avenue, New York NY 10010
Website: http://www.ibtauris.com

In the United States and Canada distributed by St. Martin's Press
175 Fifth Avenue, New York NY 10010

ISBN 1 86064 645 X

A full CIP record for this book is available from the British Library
A full CIP record for this book is available from the Library of Congress

Library of Congress catalog card: available

Typeset in Stone by Dexter Haven, London
Printed and bound in Great Britain

CONTENTS

INTRODUCTION

Critics are asked which is their favourite film, by somebody or other, about once a week. I've had my soup curdled at a good many dinner parties that way. I used to vary my reply according to mood until, tired of that, I got into the habit of simply saying Ozu's *Tokyo Story*. Most people who know their cinema nod with some approval, since *Tokyo Story* is indeed a masterpiece – probably the best, most human film ever made about family relationships. The vast majority of people, however, just shut up, since they've never heard of Yashiro Ozu and haven't seen the film. I don't blame them at all. Britain has one of the most restrictive exhibition systems in Europe, and there's little or no hope of seeing an enormous amount of world cinema, even on video or the internet.

This is the main reason I'm writing this book – to remind people that the cinema didn't start with *Star Wars* and that, during its hundred or so years of existence, it has produced as many major artists as any other art form during that time. Indeed probably more. These people should be remembered and their films shown. If they were, those fed on a remorseless diet of Hollywood pap might get a considerable shock. In my opinion, if you don't know who Ozu was, it is rather like saying: 'Who's Bach?'

If you think I'm exaggerating, let me tell you of the head of the British branch of a major American company who once rang me up and asked if I'd ever heard of a director called Brunel. 'Brunel?' I said, 'What did he make? *The Bridge*?' 'No,' he replied, 'It's a film called *The Discreet Charge of the Light Brigade*'. So much for Buñuel's *The Discreet Charm of the Bourgeoisie*. The ignorance extends wider and deeper than you think.

Any critic, however, who claims to know exactly which are the 100 best films ever made is either very brave or very foolish. Whatever some may claim, criticism is a subjective art, and even if it weren't the flowers in cinema's garden are so various that there's no such thing as one standard by which to judge them. My series in the *Guardian*, of which I was film critic for some 30 years, was indeed called 'The 100 Best'. But that was journalistic licence. My purpose was different. It was to select 100 films, seen over those thirty years, either as brand new offerings or as revivals, which I could not contemplate never seeing again. A better if more cliched title might under the circumstances have been 'Desert Island Movies'.

I did not choose the films as a group before writing about them, but gradually forged my list week by week. Clint Eastwood once told me that Don Seigel, one of his favourite film-makers, used to direct his films by osmosis. Well, that the way I selected my 100. I only had one rule, which was to select the directors I admired most and then decide which of their films was most appropriate. Each film-maker could only have one film – otherwise my favourite directors might well have landed up with four or five. It wasn't just their most famous films, but either their most typical or their most surprising. I'm aware this binds me rather tightly to the old-fashioned auteur theory. But though I believe that film is a co-operative art, and that often films are made good by their actors, cinematographers, producers and, perhaps most of all, their editors, each of the films I have selected depends first and foremost on its director.

Of course, every time I look at my list I have regrets. Why did I leave out this in favour of that? But that's inevitable, and my apologies to the British film-makers in particular whom I have failed to put in. All I would claim is that, taken together, the films I have selected will give readers a reasonable idea of what the cinema can do. Not only that, but an idea too of the huge number of countries that have produced marvellous films. The multiplexes of this country may feed us a diet of what I call McDonald's culture. But world cinema is capable of so much more than that. I'll be happy if, in between cursing me for what I've left out, readers of this book have their appetites whetted for more ambitious work and their curiosity stimulated about some of the directors I have chosen who are by no means as well known as they deserve. I believe the general run of film-goers is rather more intelligent that the distributors and exhibitors fancy. That they often want to know more but can't find out, or at least don't know where to start. I hope a few of them start here, and keep going.

JOHNNY GUITAR

Directed by Nicholas Ray
With Sterling Hayden, Joan Crawford
USA, 1954, 111 minutes

'There was theatre (Griffith), poetry (Murnau), painting (Rossellini), dance (Eisenstein), music (Renoir). Henceforward there is cinema. And the cinema is Nicholas Ray.' The quote is from Jean-Luc Godard and whether you agree or think him mildly mad, it is certainly true that those who admire Ray are often besotted enough to move inexorably towards hyperbole. Count me in as far as *Johnny Guitar* is concerned. But I'll try to contain myself.

This baroque and deliriously stylised western, along with Fritz Lang's *Rancho Notorious* and Raoul Walsh's *Pursued*, proves it is possible to lift the genre into the realms of Freudian analysis, political polemic and even Greek tragedy.

Sterling Hayden, an actor who wasn't exactly a major star but certainly had an unforgettable screen presence, is Johnny Guitar, a gunslinger who is summoned by his ex-lover Vienna (Joan Crawford) to protect her saloon from the violent opposition of the locals, who fear her plans to build a rail station.

Led by Mercedes McCambridge's Emma, who loves Scott Brady's Dancin' Kid, who in turn is obsessed with Vienna, they give her 24 hours to leave town. Finally, Emma kills the Kid and then goes after Vienna.

It is difficult to describe what makes *Johnny Guitar* so fascinating, except to say that Ray's orchestration of Philip Yordan's almost literary screenplay gives a small-budget film, made for the cheapskate Republic Studios, a kind of heady but clipped dignity which renders Truffaut's remark about a 'hallucinatory Western' seem a good deal less daft than Godard's.

On the political level, which was more important then than now, the film is a brave indictment of the McCarthyite bigotry that swept America during the fifties – an impression of the present, one American critic wrote at the time, filmed through the myths of the past.

No movie is unrelated to the time in which it was made, and every film changes when viewed from a different time. So perhaps the most affecting feature of the film now is its deep romanticism. Johnny, who no longer carries a gun, is still in love with Vienna. But she, once no better than she ought to be, is now an independent woman in control of her own destiny. If he wants her back, he's going to have to take her on her own terms. Even as he saves her from her rabid, almost pathological enemies, he knows that.

The film is infinitely detailed and infinitely complicated if you want to analyse it. It was made at a juncture in movie history when westerns were attempting to rid themselves of the Hopalong Cassidy–Roy Rogers matinee image, and it's pretty sure that Ray used Crawford, who wanted to play up rather than down-market, because he was attracted to her, like Johnny to Vienna.

What she does in the film transcends either camp or melodrama. It's like watching a legend at work throwing off her previous baggage and gaining a new acting skin. As for Hayden, his almost stiff stillness, which could be dull (in duller movies) here seems remarkable.

Of course the film is an acquired taste. Not every American film beloved by Cahiers du Cinema gets the British behind it. But there is no doubt that Ray, always a maverick and finally a tragic, neglected figure surrounded by obsequious young acolytes and filmed virtually on his deathbed by Wim Wenders in the doubtfully intrusive but admiring *Lightning Over Water*, could make great films.

For myself, *Johnny Guitar* is one of them. For all its slightly tatty sets and off-the-mark decor, the film abounds in wonderful lines and acting that doesn't betray them. Here's an example:

Johnny: How many men have you forgotten?
Vienna: As many women as you've remembered.
Johnny: Don't go away.
Vienna: I haven't moved.
Johnny: Tell me something nice.
Vienna: Sure. What do you want to hear?
Johnny: Lie to me. Tell me all these years you've waited.
Vienna: All these years I've waited.
Johnny: Tell me you'd have died if I hadn't come back.
Vienna: I would have died if you hadn't come back.
Johnny: Tell me you still love me like I love you.
Vienna: I still love you like you love me.
Johnny: Thanks. Thanks a lot.

THE TRAVELLING PLAYERS

Directed by Theo Angelopoulos
With Eva Kotamanidou, Aliki Georgoulis
Greece, 1975, 230 minutes

Of the small posse of the world's arguably great directors still with us, Theo Angelopoulos, born in Athens in 1936, is probably the least known. The reasons are obvious. He is a film-maker who flatly refuses compromise. The slow pace and austere style of his work is utterly against current trends, and the content is invariably as formidably intellectual as it is emotional and poetic. His films are, to put it bluntly, not everybody's idea of a good night out. At his best, however, he is unquestionably a master. And only the fact that he so obviously knows it renders that fact unsympathetic.

Now finally invested with the Palme d'Or at Cannes, a prize he has coveted for years, even to the extent of making a churlish speech when earlier offered the runners-up award, he seems content at last to allow history to judge his work for itself. It should certainly judge *The Travelling Players* (*O Thiassos*) as a classic.

The film was made in 1975, with some danger, during the period of the semi-fascist rule of the Colonels. Quite how the military police who watched its progress allowed it to be completed is surprising, since the film examines the turbulent history of its country from an obviously radical, almost Brechtian, point of view. Perhaps the Colonels' men thought that this story of a troupe of itinerant actors touring *Golfo the Shepherdess*, a pastoral folk drama set to music and song, was harmless enough. But it wasn't, since its period (1939–1952) warmed the seeds of their masters' military coup.

Almost four hours long, *The Travelling Players* has its actors first watch and then get caught up in the political events of the period it examines so that even their play changes its emphasis. As they progress through the often rainy and wintry provincial Greece in which Angelopoulos almost always prefers to shoot, the sequences become longer and longer and the pace seldom changes. The whole film is accomplished in around 80 shots.

But, despite that, and even though no one but a Greek can understand all the political, historical and mythic allusions, it is a fascinating progress, enlivened by Yorgos Arvanitis's often luminous photography, by Loukianos Kilaidonis's throbbing music, including songs and dances adapted from folk sources, and by performances that seem utterly truthful.

How does Angelopoulos achieve this magic? It is partly because of the utter conviction with which he steers his work towards an inner as well as an outward relevance. But take a look, if you want to see how he manages individual sequences, at the closing passage of this film, when one of the actors is executed for sedition and his fellow performers raise their hands above their heads to applaud his life at the graveside. Nothing could be done more simply – though in most successful simplicity there is a great deal of artfulness. But the sequence, perhaps because of all that has gone before, is far more moving than the myriad of funeral scenes in movies manage to be. It has a grace that is almost totally absent from most of today's cinema.

In many ways Angelopoulos has been lucky. As the outstanding Greek director, his every whim has been granted over the last half of his career by the cultural wing of the country's government. And he is clearly a difficult man to satisfy. But he has forged a unique if often pessimistic style through which to examine as minutely as he can his own country and countrymen, and sometimes even Europe itself. If you were to see all his dozen or so films, you would not only have a much greater appreciation of Greek and Balkan conflicts but a deeper view of the inner turmoil of individuals whose lives have been altered by them.

THE CROWD

Directed by King Vidor
With James Murray, Eleanor Boardman, Bert Roach
USA, 1928, 98 minutes

Not every film with an important place in the history of the cinema now looks as good as it once did. Sometimes the progress it prompted makes it seem antiquated. But King Vidor's silent *The Crowd*, made way back in 1928, is one of the exceptions which proves the rule. It's one of the first Hollywood dramas that attempted to tell us about the trials and tribulations of the ordinary American and, even now, remains one of the best.

Some thought it bitter and fundamentally unpatriotic. But it was audacious enough to attempt something like the truth at the time of the jazz era when it was thought nobody wanted to hear it. It was, however, the way it told the truth that really matters.

Consider the opening sequence, described in the director's own words.

> We showed a group of people entering and leaving a large office building in downtown New York; then the camera tilted up framing a design of multitudinous windows and dislosing the great height of the structure. The camera travelled up the building, passing many floors and windows, until it stopped at one floor and moved into one window.
>
> Through the window one can discern hundreds of desks and clerks. The camera moved through the window and started an angled descent toward one desk and one clerk – our hero concentrating on his monotonous duties. This camera manoeuvre was designed to illustrate our theme – one of the mob, one of the crowd.

There are other famous sequences, which include the crowd's seeming indifference to the death of one of the clerk's children, and his final quasi-triumph over a life that delivers much less than he might have been entitled to hope if he believed in any form of the American dream.

Actually the film was released with two endings. But Vidor's preferred one has the clerk and his wife enjoying themselves at a variety theatre, laughing at a clown, dressed as one of the unemployed he himself had been in the course of the story. Then the camera pulls back, losing him once again in the crowd.

The whole atmosphere of the film makes the clerk's progress through life in the anonymous city hardly one to be celebrated, even though his fundamental courage can be. But that is only one half of the daring of *The Crowd*, which brought to Hollywood the kind of concern about the alienation of urban living that had informed a number of the best German films of the period – and was later to be counteracted by the optimism of

European immigrants like Capra in films such as *Mr Deeds Goes To Town*. The other concerns its technique, since Vidor's fluid camera combined the best of European expressionism with the more 'natural' realism Hollywood film-makers sought to catch. The film, though, was not some one-off classic. Vidor had previously made *The Big Parade*, an almost equally good but very different film set during the First World War. And he was to continue with a series of great, or at least notable, films that had at their centre ordinary people made unordinary through their circumstances.

Perhaps the most striking was the almost baroque *The Fountainhead*, in which Gary Cooper played an ambitious architect modelled on Frank Lloyd Wright. But there was *Our Daily Bread*, *Ruby Gentry*, *Stella Dallas* and *Duel in the Sun* too. Hollywood directors like Vidor are still underrated as skilful mechanics who had the luck to work with the best technicians and actors within the studio system. But look at *The Crowd* and you'll see a genuine artist at work.

THE PASSENGER

Directed by Michelangelo Antonioni
With Jack Nicholson, Maria Schneider
Italy/France/Spain, 1975, 119 minutes

It was once said that one admires Michelangelo Antonioni's films without feeling fond of them, or one resists them, turning a blind eye to their beauty. It has also been said that his films teach us to see as we've never seen before. There's an element of truth in both statements, particularly as far as his great trilogy of *L'Avventura*, *La Notte* and *L'Eclisse* are concerned.

Each of these remarkable works, made in the early sixties, are deeply pessimistic love stories, disorienting because conventional narrative is always avoided and it often seems that nothing whatever is happening except within the minds, or possibly the confused souls, of the participants.

L'Avventura, another commentator has written, 'could never have taken place except within the anaemic milieu of the Italian bourgeoisie'. While Jeanne Moreau, who starred with Marcello Mastroianni as the loveless couple in *La Notte*, once said to me: 'God, I was bored. But you can't argue with Antonioni. He never replies.' Even so, the three films are revolutionary in form, surprisingly eloquent in content and, if you are so disposed, can effect you as deeply as any. Is he the Henry James of film-making?

It's a bit unorthodox to prefer the much later *The Passenger*, and probably says more about me than the film – the alternative title is *Profession: Reporter*. But it too is a remarkable work and a major return to form after the

incoherence and shallowness of *Zabriskie Point*, Antonioni's first American film. It is a bit like a heavily intellectualised Graham Greene story, partly because of a screenplay by Mark Peploe and the structuralist critic Peter Wollen (once a political correspondent in foreign parts) and partly because Antonioni, though not filled with Catholic guilt like Greene, was concerned like him with some sort of at least identifiably spiritual values.

In the film, Jack Nicholson plays a burnt-out television reporter who exchanges his identity with that of a man he finds dead in a North African hotel room. He does this to get away from the mess of his old life but discovers to his chagrin that he is being haunted not only by a wife and friends but by strangers he realises are not going to do him any good. He starts a relationship with Maria Schneider's younger woman, but the further he goes to get away from his previous life and his gun-running hunters, the worse the situation becomes. And he ends up sharing the same fate as the man whose mask he has taken.

The film is beautifully shot by Luciano Tovoli in France, Spain and North Africa and intimates as much about the political situation in which the reporter has been involving himself – a first world embattled with radical forces no one knows a great deal about in the Third – as it does about the state of its protagonist's mind. It also contains several amazing sequences, including a seven-minute-long penultimate take that has seldom been equalled.

It's is a travelling shot that passes through the narrow bars of a window to frame Nicholson, moves into a courtyard and then moves back to look through the bars again. The first time we see Nicholson, he is alive. The second time he is dead.

Curiously, at one point in the film, Schneider finds a gun in Nicholson's luggage and he takes it from her with a gruff 'No'. It fits the film, but it also fits the fact that Schneider shot Marlon Brando in *The Last Tango*, the film which made her famous. One dead star was perhaps enough for one so young.

Antonioni, however, is not known for his humour but for his innate capacity to express alienation visually rather than in any other way. *The Passenger* does that, so does *Blow-Up* and, of course, the aforementioned trilogy. The comparison has to be with painting, but it is also with a novelist's ability to describe as both a scene and a state of mind. If he's not particularly fashionable now, that's our loss not his.

THE GOSPEL ACCORDING TO ST MATTHEW

Directed by Pier Paolo Pasolini
With Enrique Irazoqui, Margherita Caruso
Italy/France, 1964, 142 minutes

Films about the Christian God are not exactly my cup of tea, being either maudlin and sentimental or boringly dignified, and almost always badly acted. Who can ever forget Jeffrey Hunter in *King of Kings*, who caused the film to be nicknamed 'I Was a Teenage Jesus'?

But two of them at least are memorable – Monty Python's *Life Of Brian*, which, as well as being very funny, had the added advantage of being objected to by people like Rank, and Pasolini's *The Gospel According to St Matthew*, made by a Marxist frequently accused of blasphemy by the Catholic Church, and whose attitude to religion was at best ambivalent.

Its portrait of the Messiah, played by Enrique Irazoqui, a young Spanish economics student with a now fashionable scraggy beard, is far harsher than that of the usual soft saint, and he clearly has a temper on him. He is, as Paul Mayersberg has suggested, 'a procurer for God'. But hardly a conventionally saintly one. Physically, the actor wears no make-up, and neither do the rest of the cast. Judas is played by a truck-driver from Rome (Otello Sestili) and Pasolini's own mother is the Virgin Mary. They are all amateurs, and the close-ups of their faces, untramelled by any star persona, make the story seem much more real than usual.

The bleak hillside scenery of Calabria, where the film was made, gives the film a primitive feel that is augmented by rough and grainy cinematography. The music of Prokofiev, Bach, Mozart and even Billie Holiday surprises us on the sound-track and is occasionally off-putting considering the naturalism of the scene and playing. What Pasolini clearly wanted was a believable Gospel, armed with real people and not actors filled with puffed-up sanctity.

The glories of the music sometimes work against this, since sublimity is not what Pasolini had in mind. He did say, however, that he was not interested in deconsecrating. 'That is a fashion I hate – I want to reconsecrate as much as possible'.

It's a stark film that someone has described as one-dimensional and 'a cup of bitter absinthe' but, culled from the most humane of the Gospels, it carries with it not only an authenticity but also clear-headed interpretative qualities that completely avoid the usual cliches. This Christ was a political animal, angry at social injustice. Even the silent cry from the cross seems more believable. There are no lines like 'God, thy will is hard, but you hold every card' that disfigure *Jesus Christ Superstar*, and the miracles avoid any kind of underlining comment. They just happen, with not a special effect in sight.

All this puzzled the Catholic Church greatly. But it was eventually decided to approve of the film from a man who, though he had vastly annoyed the Papacy with his episode in the earlier *RoGoPaG* with his parody of the Deposition from the Cross, and had been given a suspended prison sentence for 'publically undermining the religion of the state', had at least had the grace to be expelled from the Communist Party, albeit for alleged homosexuality.

A planned life of St Paul never materialised, and instead we had the less ambitious but more popular entertainment of *The Decameron*, *The Canterbury Tales* and *The Arabian Nights* and the more intellectual, poetic and at times portentous *Hawks and Sparrows*, *Theorem*, *Pigsty* and *Medea*.

He never acquired the purity of *The Gospel* again, and *Salo*, his last film, went precisely in the opposite direction – a tortured scream against Fascism that almost succeeded in being fascist itself. He was a loved and sometimes hated seminal figure of Italian culture so that his murder, almost certainly by a teenage hustler, was and still is interpreted by many as some sort of political conspiracy.

A BOUT DE SOUFFLE

Directed by Jean-Luc Godard
With Jean-Paul Belmondo, Jean Seberg
France, 1960, 89 minutes

There could hardly be a more fascinating, or exasperating, film-maker than Jean-Luc Godard. His work, now spanning 40 years, has probably been more influential than that of any other post-war director. Yet, though he was once popular, at least with a public prepared to invest in sub-titled films, his later films are now anathema at the box-office practically everywhere. Not that he seems to mind overmuch. He's been cocking a snook at us for some considerable time.

This being so, and granted that he has made an enormous number of different and often contradictory films, we might as well start at his extraordinary beginning – *A Bout de Souffle* (*Breathless*). It reached us like a clap of thunder in 1960, immediately establishing an international reputation and introducing us to a new kind of paradoxical hero who has been copied, usually badly, ever since. 'Squealers squeal, burglars burgle, killers kill, lovers love,' he says to his American girlfriend. In other words, what we are determines what we do.

Michel (Belmondo) is a small-time hood and a killer. He's just murdered a policeman and goes to Paris to collect enough money to leave the country, trying to persuade his girl (Jean Seberg) to go with him. She, however, is playing at being the American intellectual in Paris and, when he finally gets his money, betrays him to the police. That's the narrative, if you can call it such. But Godard is not interested in telling us a story, or even in character development. Instead, he relies on a free-wheeling camera style, rambling conversations, incongruous incidents, jump-cuts and iconic bows to the American cinema he loved and hated at the same time.

Michel thinks he's a French version of Humphrey Bogart, Seberg's Patricia is much like the Seberg of Preminger's *Bonjour Tristesse* but even more phoney. And Godard himself mimics the Sam Fuller of *Forty Guns* at one point. The whole thing is playful and deadly serious at the same time. Playful because Godard can never resist teasing parody, and serious because he was making an earnest enough statement about deconstructing the usual film forms. Images and sounds create meaning, but not in the order they are usually manufactured.

What we also learn from the film is that you can construct an effective image of contemporary life not just with location shooting but with a kind of cultural collage of movie posters, art reproductions, magazines and books.

All this, of course, is old hat by now. But it was a new one when Godard first tried it, rendering the film puzzling even to those who admired its liveliness, irony and pawky humour. The film is deeply romantic too, since it contrasts the essential honesty of Michel, faced by a senseless, fractured world and the girl's lack of commitment to anything, even him. 'C'est vraiment degueulasse' ('You really are a little bitch') are his last words to her as he lies dying in the street from a police bullet. 'Qu'est-ce que c'est, degueulasse?' she replies.

After *A Bout de Souffle*, the fragmentation of narrative became more and more audacious and the films, though frequently brilliant, like *Vivre Sa Vie*, *Alphaville* or *Pierrot Le Fou*, become less and less capable of even being analysed in a conventional way. Someone has described them as mosaics gone mad. Later still they also became more overtly political, more determined to deny art and, with the failure of Marxism, more deeply pessimistic.

Is Godard the great director we once thought? Certainly many of his later films, which often seem to deny his own virtues as a film-maker, make it possible to decry him. But he has spent his life confronting issues central to the future of cinema and, in general, to the world we live in. Besides, *A Bout de Souffle* and its successors, at least up to the end of the sixties, will certainly live as long as the cinema does.

ASHES AND DIAMONDS

Directed by Andrzej Wajda
With Zbigniew Cybulski, Ewa Krzyzewska
Poland, 1958, 106 minutes

There was a time, and it now seems long ago – thanks to the advent of capitalism and the exigencies of having to make market-driven films – when the Polish cinema was admired throughout Europe and the West. It was characterised by a deep sense of a fractured national identity, and by an extraordinarily sharp idea of how a tragic history affected ordinary people.

This renaissance, deep in the Stalinist period of the fifties, was substantially due to the emergence of a world-class director in Andrzej Wajda, whose wartime trilogy of *A Generation*, *Kanal* and *Ashes and Diamonds* remains one of the finest achievements of Eastern European cinema.

A Generation is about a group of young men and women fighting in occupied Poland, *Kanal* is the terrible story of the final abortive Warsaw uprising. But arguably the greatest of these was *Ashes and Diamonds*, in

which Zbigniew Cybulski became a star, almost in the mould of a European James Dean.

Maciek is a young soldier in the right-wing Nationalist Army ordered, at the conclusion of the war, to assassinate the newly arrived Communist District Secretary. He is a slightly dandified Polish Hamlet who has fought in the uprising but now remains uncertain about continuing to espouse an inevitably lost cause against the left. What's more, he bungles the murder, killing two innocent bystanders.

Told to try again, he is hopelessly riven between the demands of conscience and loyalty, and further upended by falling for a girl in the hotel at which he and the Communist official are staying. She makes him feel that his lifestyle is now meaningless in the new post-war atmosphere.

Though he manages to accomplish his mission on the very evening that fireworks announce the end of hostilities – ironically as his elderly prey is on his way to see his son, arrested as a member of a similar underground group to his own – he is accidentally shot when running from a passing military patrol. He dies alone on a rubbish dump in a scene reminiscent of Buñuel's *Los Olvidados*.

Cybulski manages, through Wajda, to express not only a uniquely Polish sensibility, aware of the hard history of his nation, but also the kind of youthful frustrations that apply even today. But Wajda's deeply romantic and personal vision, inspired by both Italian neo-realism and by the more baroque images of expressionism, makes *Ashes and Diamonds* a holding experience too. Once again, as in most of my 100 films, it is the cinematographer as much as the director who should be praised. Jerzy Wojcil's plastic work is outstanding.

Wajda once said to me, when I asked whether he would prefer the freedom of western film-making to the artistic constraints of the Eastern bloc, that there were always ways of getting round political censorship, but none of avoiding the censorship of money. Later in his career, he showed with *Man of Iron, Man of Marble* and several other outstanding films, when his disillusionment with the Communist Party was complete, exactly what he meant.

Ashes and Diamonds is not without irony, such as the moment when Maciek and the Party official fall almost ludicrously into each other's arms as the one kills the other; and the victory banquet at the hotel where the polonaise 'Farewell, My Homeland' is played and where some know their careers are at an end while others prepare to accept government posts in Warsaw.

The title of the novel by Jerzy Andrzejewski, who also wrote the screenplay of the film, comes from romantic poetry: 'Will there remain among the ashes a star-like diamond, the dawn of eternal victory?' Wajda doesn't attempt to answer the question. And it is the film's ambiguities, as the film-maker tries to come to grips with the myths and legends of the era, that continue to render it fascinating.

THE LEOPARD

Directed by Luchino Visconti
With Burt Lancaster, Alain Delon, Claudia Cardinale
Italy, 1963, 205 minutes

Visconti was the aristocrat of the Italian cinema, who was also an avowed Marxist. That fact alone makes his films intriguing, none more so than *The Leopard*, one of the grandest of widescreen historical epics starring Burt Lancaster as Prince Salina, the Sicilian leopard of the title. He is an ageing patrician whose declining fortunes under the upstart Garibaldi and the Risorgimento of the 1860s lead him to arrange a financially advantageous marriage between his nephew Tancredi (Alain Delon) and the daughter of a rich merchant (Claudia Cardinale).

Lancaster, at first sight an eccentric choice, not only carries all before him in the part but often said he based it on Visconti himself – a man who acknowledged the need for change but increasingly began to regret the vulgarity of the present compared with the past. Oddly, vulgarity is what Visconti's critics accuse him of, because of the operatic conception of many of his movies, their opulence of tone and their obsessively decorated appearance.

Visconti came to the fore in the forties with *Obssessione*, adopting the precepts of the neo-realist movement but adding a melodramatic, formalised structure. Later he was to reject neo-realism completely in favour of a more classical tradition which seemed to defend the humanist literary tradition. *The Leopard*, for instance, was taken from the novel by Lampedusa which sought to ruminate on the old versus the new, and to suggest that the best values of the past were equal and in some ways superior to those of the eager, pseudo-revolutionary present.

Fixing this conception with a gimlet eye, Visconti ends his film with a virtually hour-long ball scene, in which all his visual powers are in evidence and also his philosophical doubts and ruminations. The Leopard has to accept that the old order is finished and power has finally and irrevocably passed to the *nouveau riche* of the world. It is a stunning set piece that has very probably never been equalled, and the film won the Palme d'Or at Cannes.

Unfortunately it was financed by 20th Century Fox, who, despite its European acclaim, butchered it comprehensively, releasing a much shorter version that was dubbed and reprocessed as well. It took 20 years before a fully restored version was made available and a classic was seen as it should have been.

Visconti had enormous help in making the film from his cinematographer Giuseppe Rotunno and from Nino Rota, whose music is equally apt. Rotunno's ability to change the mood of scenes with expressive lighting, his ability to show us precisely the time of day, and his eloquent sense of colour gave an epic film the intimacy it needed.

But its glories are mostly Visconti's, largely because his talents suited the subject so well. There is a sensuousness about the direction which perfectly matched the ideas behind the film, the most sophisticated of which was that, even when the old order was able to reach an accommodation with the new, it brought a kind of corrupting decadence with it. Only the Prince escapes this charge because he eventually recognises this bitter truth.

All this was very different from the orthodox Marxism of films like *La Terra Trema*. But then Visconti was as full of ambiguities as many of his films. The world for him was a kind of melodrama in which passion and destiny predominated. And frequently the radical nature of what he was trying to say was almost obliterated by the way he said it. In *The Leopard* the two came together superbly. Now we can see it properly, it is probably his greatest film.

OH, MR PORTER!

Directed by Marcel Varnel
With Will Hay, Graham Moffatt, Moore Marriott
UK, 1937, 85 minutes

One of the biggest successes at the Paris Cinémathèque in the late eighties was a retrospective of British comedy curated by Bertrand Tavernier. Among the discoveries for the French was Will Hay, who with his henchmen Graham Moffatt (the fat boy) and Moore Marriott (the wizened old codger) perfectly represented a certain type of bumbling British humour.

One of the best of their films was *Oh, Mr Porter!* and the French were pleased to find it was directed by Marcel Varnel, one of their own filmmakers. Will Hay often used to play, in the music halls, on radio and on film, a genteel and pompous schoolmaster, permanently sniffing and wiping his nose, who invariably got himself into difficulties of his own making but somehow managed to get out of them by luck rather than judgement.

Moffatt was equally incompetent and the rueful butt of his jokes, while Marriott seemed the epitome of virtually senile density. In the almost equally good *Convict 99*, Marriott appeared as a long-term prisoner who spent years digging an underground tunnel, only to find, when he attempted to reach the surface, that he was in the middle of the warden's office. I seem to recall that all he said was 'Damnation!' as he attempted to scuttle back down again.

In *Oh, Mr Porter!*, however, Hay plays a railway porter with ambitions of becoming a stationmaster. Somehow he manages to get himself appointed to the virtually derelict station of Buggleskelly in Ireland where Albert (Moffatt) and old Jeremiah Harbottle are his assistants.

Desperate to justify himself, Hay organises a day excursion but manages to get mixed up with gun-runners. He fortuitously captures them after a long locomotive chase and, once again, becomes a hero despite himself. There is a wonderful windmill sequence as a climax to the film which has everyone hanging on for grim death but never quite falling.

Varnel pursues the course of this silly story with considerable vigour, timing the gags well and watching closely as Hay, Moffatt and Marriott spit out their double-talk routines, taken directly from the music hall, as to the manor born, mocking as they do so a dozen or so sacred cows of the day, from the police to imperialism.

Hay's films were made between 1934 and 1943 and helped to lay the ground for the post-war Ealing comedies, which were considerably richer in cinematic invention and subsidiary characterisation but often not as sharp about the Britain we now love to be nostalgic about.

DEREK MALCOLM'S PERSONAL BEST

His characters were oblivious to irony, serious-minded nincompoops who never learnt their lesson, escaping from calamity by sheer good fortune and then claiming they knew how to do so all along. His signature was total hypocrisy but, though hardly possessed of a single identifiable virtue, you couldn't help liking him.

Hay, Moffatt and Marriott together were a trio now largely forgotten. But like Old Mother Riley and her daughter Kitty (Arthur Lucan and Kitty McShane), they formed part of a British comedy scene which successfully translated itself from stage to screen and became part and parcel of everybody's consciousness, particularly in the war years.

DAY OF WRATH

Directed by Carl Dreyer
With Thorkild Roose, Lizbeth Movin
Denmark, 1943, 105 minutes

It is quite common to hear film buffs, even critics, acknowledge Carl Dreyer's greatness with the merest hint of a yawn, as if this Danish director of *The Passion of Joan of Arc*, *Vampyr*, *Ordet and Gertrud* was a film-maker relevant to history but not to us today.

Yet Godard paid tribute to him in *Vivre Sa Vie* when Anna Karina is moved to tears by Falconetti in *The Passion of Joan of Arc*, and Antonioni, Resnais and other directors who came into prominence in the sixties freely acknowledge their stylistic and moral debt to him.

Nothing could be further from the truth than characterising him as a close relative to Shakespeare's gloomy Dane and his films as too slow and lingering, too concerned with martyrdom and suffering and too intent on marketing a gaunt spirituality to reach out to modern audiences. *Vampyr*, for instance, was one of the most poetic horror films ever made, and *Day of Wrath* one of the most physically terrifying.

The fact is that almost all his films, stretching through the silent era into sound, etch themselves in the memory. And if they deal with the kind of subject matter today's film-makers, and some audiences, find largely beyond them, that is surely not to his discredit. He stands amongst the greatest, most profound artists of the twentieth century.

Day of Wrath is about the persecution of witches in the seventeenth century and is sometimes seen as an allegory on the German occupation of Denmark. Anne, the second wife of an old pastor, has given refuge to an alleged witch, and discovers that her own mother, also accused of witchcraft, was saved from the stake by the pastor in exchange for her

hand. Falling in love with her stepson, she is wracked with guilt and confesses to her husband. When he dies from the shock, she herself is denounced as a witch and burnt at the stake.

The film, in looks sometimes reminiscent of Dutch painting, examines the tortuous cruelty of the time, supposed to be the workings of divine law, and also the two central characters – one of whom admits under torture that she is a witch and the other who volunteers to die, convinced of her own evil.

Dreyer's measured pace and stark visuals – long horizontal pans and close-ups of riven faces – accompanied as they are by acting of intense realism, make this a morality play of enormous power. And the scenes of torture and burning, though discreetly handled, are almost unbearable, at least partly because the torturers and burners are not mere hysterics but stolidly convinced they have divine justice on their side.

What Dreyer achieves is the sense that, for these sternly Protestant people, their inscrutable faces concealing great passion, witchcraft was a frightening reality. He does not argue for or against it but simply, as a critic has said, evokes the dark night of the soul through an intensely physical world.

Most directors refine their style towards the end of their lives, and Dreyer did so with *Gertrud*, which some regard as one of the dozen or so greatest films ever made and others as an impenetrable bore; just as *The Passion of Joan of Arc* is regarded either as a masterpiece of the silent cinema or a film saved by the luminous face of Falconetti. Dreyer was indeed not everybody's director. He was, however, over some 45 years of work, a unique and innovating talent.

JULES ET JIM

Directed by François Truffaut
With Jeanne Moreau, Oskar Werner, Henri Serre
France, 1962, 110 minutes

One of the most remarkable things about François Truffaut's *Jules et Jim*, now regarded as the audacious apotheosis of the French New Wave, is that it was adapted from a novel written by a seventy-five-year-old writer. What we think of now as a perennially 'young' film was thus the product of an old man's sensibility. Henri-Pierre Roche died, in fact, just before Truffaut went into production.

Despite this, Truffaut regarded the book as an example of the kind of story that would never have been made by the 'Cinema of Quality' which the critics and film-makers of the New Wave considered reactionary and moribund. And he adapted it with the exceptional panache and flair that was often not present in his later films, despite their other virtues. While it wasn't characteristic of the two earlier films of Truffaut himself, and certainly not of Godard and Chabrol's first efforts, it was at least as daring and definitely richer and more mature.

The film chonicles some twenty years in the lives of its three central characters, starting off in the era of La Belle Epoque, just before the First World War, and ending at the time of the Great Depression and the rise of Hitler. And what is so astonishing about it is not just its freshness and vitality – the feeling that life is always exciting if sometimes dangerous – but the way the young director managed to mould his characters so accurately to the events of their time.

He did this with the aid of copious references to old movies, photographs and slides, paintings, novels, music and theatre. Few other films, before or since, illustrate better the axiom that the best film-makers have to know something about all the arts rather than just film. But, of course, it is the changing reactions of the *ménage-à-trois* to each other that most of us remember.

Although the film is called *Jules et Jim*, the dominant character in it is Catherine, who fascinates them like the statue of the stone goddess they have admired earlier. She is independent and unpredictable, and silly enough to throw herself into the Seine when the two men discuss a Strindberg play without her participation. She is prepared to be courted by Jules and to bear him a child but not ready to be either an orthodox wife or mother. She even starts an affair with Jim, half knowing that both men are too fond of each other and of her to break off their friendship. Besides, as she says, 'One is never completely in love for more than a moment'.

Jeanne Moreau was the perfect choice for Catherine, and gives a performance full of gaiety and charm but also manages to convey a sense that she is the opposite of an attractive but empty-headed bimbo. She makes the watcher understand that this is no ordinary woman whom both men adore. It is possibly the most complete and holding portrait of any feminine character in the entire *ouevre* of the New Wave, and it made her an international star.

The film is full of idyllic moments which transform, as suddenly as they began, into doubt and retreat. The atmosphere of gathering gloom with which the film ends is thus totally logical, matching the storm clouds over Europe. 'They left nothing behind them' is the commentary's epitaph after the death of Catherine. The whirlwind of life about which she has so often sung continues, but without the three friends.

Jules et Jim seemed revolutionary at the time, and remains so even now in some senses, despite the fact that bits and pieces of it have been copied again and again. But then Truffaut's revolution, unlike Godard's, implied not so much the destruction of the past as a turning back to the humanism of Vigo and Renoir and the French cinema of the thirties. The 'rondo of love' of this remarkable film represents both a backward glance at the best of the past and a forward glance into the cinema's future. Basically, its enthusiasm for what the cinema is and can be is what makes it so special.

FANTASIA

Walt Disney Productions
USA, 1940, 120 minutes

'Dull as it is towards the end, ridiculous as it is in the bend of the knee before Art, and taking one thing with another, it is one of the strange and beautiful things that have happened in the world.' Thus spake Otis Ferguson, the American reviewer, of Walt Disney's *Fantasia*, one of the most admired and also one of the most reviled animation features ever made. And them's my sentiments exactly. Notwithstanding the fact that I wince whenever I see the dreadful cuteness contained within the section devoted to Beethoven's Pastoral Symphony and cringe at the awe-inspiring religiosity of the 'Ave Maria' conclusion to 'Night On Bare Mountain' (Moussorgsky mated with Schubert). There are other passages I'll never forget for better reasons.

Of course, I'm still seeing it with a child's eye, since that was when I was first introduced to this incredibly bold adventure. Even so, the wonderfully kitsch 'Nutcracker Suite', the extraordinary pyrotechnics of Dukas's 'The Sorcerer's Apprentice', the witty anthropomorphism of Ponticelli's 'Dance of the Hours' and the brave attempt to illustrate Bach's Toccata and Fugue in D Minor in abstract form render *Fantasia* an undoubted milestone in animation.

To Disney, it was the most ambitious of his experiments in technique. To Leopold Stokowski, the conductor of the Philadelphia Orchestra, it was a 'concert feature' attempting to popularise classical music. To Stravinsky, whose *Rite of Spring* was restructured, and then made to illustrate what someone described as a 'paleontological cataclysm of ponderous didacticism', it was torment – 'I'll say nothing about the visual complement as I do not wish to criticise an unresisting imbecility'.

All very American, in fact, paying obeisance to culture without a proper understanding of it and only at its best when playing rude games with art. The games, however, are pretty marvellous. And who understands culture properly anyway? Perhaps Beethoven would have laughed instead of swivelling in his grave.

The reason for much of the still vocal opposition is almost certainly because of Disney's success in not only influencing the course of animation but infecting us all with his grossly sentimental and often reactionary values. He, and his successors at the factory, have become the McDonald's of cinema. 'Our environment, our sensibilities, the very quality of both our waking and sleeping hours, are all formed largely by people with no more artistic conscience and intelligence than a kumquat,' wrote Richard Schickel.

What we should also remember, however, is that Disney was once heralded as a serious artist rather than just a superb craftsman, and praised by no lesser figure than Eisenstein as 'the most interesting director in America'. But after the failure of *Fantasia* (shortlived since the film has now gone well into profit), Disney decided that 'We're through with caviar. From now on it's mashed potatoes and gravy'.

Fantasia is mashed potatoes and gravy but there's more than a hint of Beluga there too. You don't catch too many children these days reading *Wind in the Willows*. But you can't stop most of them watching *Fantasia*. Why? Because Disney's story-telling, rather lost in the new *Fantasia 2000*, was unbeatable for a start. He was also a supreme innovator and perfectionist who never ceased to explore the possibilities of the medium.

If Disneyland and Disneyworld are ghastly monuments to his successors' gifts as organisers and publicists, his best films remain much more than his limited sensibilities would seem to suggest possible.

NANOOK OF THE NORTH

Directed by Robert Flaherty
USA, 1922, 75 minutes

We have become so accustomed to television documentaries in which someone famous travels to a distant part of the world to view its inhabitants in their natural state, or to nature programmes in which a distinguished and actorly voice-over lends weight to the cameramen's patient skills, that we have quite forgotten from whence it all originated. One of the fountainheads was Robert Flaherty, an American from Michigan who was as much the great Victorian romantic as any Englishman born in the late nineteenth century.

Flaherty was a pioneer of the documentary form and one of those whose work first sparked many of the arguments about truth and falsehood within the genre which still cause friction today, particularly on television where blatant set-ups try to persuade us of some general truth. For this reason, his style is now often patronised as naive and schematic at the

same time. But if you look at *Nanook of the North*, his first major film about Eskimo life, you can see where so much else has come from.

The son of a miner, he first tried exploring and map-making with the Canadian Northern Railway and then decided upon revealing on film the Eskimo life he had first found on Baffin Island. The filming was done over almost two years on the eastern shore of Hudson Bay, and Flaherty's objective was complete authenticity. He wielded his gyroscope camera himself, taking along into his harsh surroundings enough equipment to process and develop the film and to show it to the Eskimos themselves.

Nanook and his family were real. But not all their everyday life was filmed as it took place. They amiably enacted some of it for Flaherty's cameras, regarding him as a kind of Great White Father who would tell the world about their ceaseless hunt for food and their hard-fought battle against nature. This was often the reverse of *cinema verité*. But so honest and instinctive was their playing that it was undoubtedly truth of a sort.

The background comes to the fore, and that is real enough, photographed in black-and-white with consummate dramatic skill. And though the film has no conventional plot, it manages to tell a coherent story solely through its extraordinary images. It hints at that old cliche about the noble savage, gradually being pushed towards a civilisation that will somehow destroy him. But it does so with a rare feeling for a timeless landscape and a way of life that had at that time remained the same for centuries.

The building of the igloo out of ice and snow is perhaps the most famous and fascinating episode. It is taken step by step without the explanation that might render it more mundane today, though the way translucent blocks of ice are used as windows could hardly seem humdrum in any hands. But again Flaherty 'cheated', since he had an igloo constructed to twice the normal size, with half of it cut away to provide more light for the negative stock in his camera.

When the film was released, it got rave reviews and no one called it a documentary. It seemed at the time simply in a class by itself. It still is. Flaherty was never again to achieve such a lack of self-consciousness and purity of style, though films like *Moana*, about the Samoan lifestyle, *Man of Aran* and *Louisiana Story* contained extraordinary sequences.

He had what was once called 'an innocent eye' which tried to discover 'the elemental truths that all men share'. He was naive, patrician, eccentric, obdurate, and had the eye of a painter – perhaps the attributes of many good film-makers. He believed that if Eskimos could tame nature, then the rest of us could tame our more advanced civilisation. Perversely, *Nanook of the North* was made for a fur-trading company. Perversely also, it was Nanook himself rather than the film-maker who became an instant celebrity.

VERTIGO

Directed by Alfred Hitchcock
With James Stewart, Kim Novak
USA, 1958, 127 minutes

It doesn't seem so very long ago that Alfred Hitchcock was considered not much more than a superior craftsman specialising in slightly glib thrillers the public liked. A very superior craftsman, perhaps, but scarcely a real artist. Now, of course, the critical wheel has turned full circle. Hitch is dubbed a master, and a round dozen of his films are regarded as classics. They are.

One of them, made in the late fifties, is *Vertigo*, and the strangest, most perverse movie he ever made. It was never really popular except with the critics. But for once one can confidently say they were right. And those who did see and like it were probably as emotionally moved by it as by any other Hitchcock film.

The story, as if you could forget it, has James Stewart as Scotty, a private eye cursed with a pathological fear of heights since being held responsible for the fatal fall of a fellow officer in the days when he was in the police. Hired to protect a threatened woman (Kim Novak), his 'weakness', as the coroner puts it, stops him saving her from a suicidal leap. We know he was also in love with her.

When he comes out of the institution in which he is undergoing treatment, he meets another woman who reminds him of his dead love (actually it is the same one, since her death was fabricated as cover for a murder). Obsessively, he tries to make the woman reassemble her previous incarnation – 'Couldn't you like me, just me, the way I am?' she says after an uncomfortable shopping expedition during which he tries to dress her up like his former love.

What he wants seems to be what Hitch himself always wanted – a blonde ice goddess. And the film fits perfectly into its director's own view of sexuality, which seldom reaches further down than to an unrequited obsession that virtually deranges those in thrall to it.

But the film isn't just about that. Scotty and his woman are caught up in more than their slightly lunatic affair. The plot twists and turns around the original murder with almost Gothic abandon until its famous, and superbly shot and edited, climax in the bell-tower.

You could call *Rear Window*, *Vertigo* and *Psycho* an unequalled trilogy about voyeurism or, if you want to be more orthodox, a set of films forcing ordinary audiences to admit their very unordinary fears. His great films, as the critic David Thompson says, are only partly his. They also belong to the minds of those who interpret them.

However you look at them – and there are about a dozen different ways – they do at least prove that Hitch was a director whose art contained considerably more than a vast knowledge of the tricks of his trade and a consuming ambition to play on the susceptibilities of his audiences. There is a coldness alongside his calculations, it is true. Misanthropy surfaces too – look at the way he treats Midge, the woman who truly loves Scotty in *Vertigo*.

But the essential greatness, sometimes amounting to genius, remains. You can see it as well as anywhere else in *Vertigo*, made all the more noteworthy by Bernard Herrmann's ghost-ridden score, Robert Burks's sharp-etched cinematography and, above all, the scaled-down eloquence of James Stewart's central performance.

It is difficult to see who could equal Hitchcock in his chosen teasing and ironic idiom, or whom one could admire more as a film-maker. It is easy enough, however, to find directors one likes more. *Vertigo* is a great film. But for me it couldn't stand comfortably beside something like Renoir's *Rules of the Game*. Conjurors are not often comfortable as philosophers.

BOY

Directed by Nagisa Oshima
With Fumio Watanabe, Akiko Koyama
Japan, 1969, 97 minutes

Nagisa Oshima is most widely known in the West for *In the Realm of the Senses*, a story of sexual obsession, based on a true incident, which had censors everywhere reaching for their scissors. The fact that the film was also a metaphor for the militarist ills of Japan escaped them entirely. But Oshima shouldn't be judged solely on the audacity and shock tactics of this admittedly astonishing film.

He was, in fact, only one of three outstanding film-makers who reacted against the classical, humanist cinema of Ozu, Mizoguchi and Kurosawa and determined to delve into the structures of Japanese society as they were being broken down in the modern world. The other two were Imamura and Shinoda who, like Oshima, were deeply affected by the French New Wave in their struggle against the studio system in Japan. It's difficult to say who was the most successful, but each made unforgettable films totally different to the great Japanese movies of the fifties.

Oshima's *Death by Hanging, Diary of a Shinjuku Thief* and *The Ceremony* showed an even firmer grasp than *In the Realm of the Senses* of the way Japan was changing and the profound effect of that change. But my favourite of his films is *Boy*, taken directly, like *Realm*, from newspaper clippings.

The film illustrates perfectly the view all three of these very different film-makers had about the underbelly of Japan. Which was that it was often worth studying much more than conventional society, and that its denizens deserved as much sympathy and understanding as anybody else. The lovers in *Realm* were outsiders, and so is the down-and-out itinerant family depicted in this far less notorious but equally impressive film.

The father is lazy and embittered, the step-mother more presentable in a tarty sort of way, ever hopeful that father's ten-year-old son will regard her with affection. The only way they can think of making a living is by using the boy as a breadwinner. He has to fake being injured in road accidents in order to blackmail 'hospital money' out of the frightened drivers.

It's a strategy that has some success until, perhaps inevitably, the boy is caught. But despite his confusion and his obvious unhappiness, he refuses to admit anything to the police. His loyalty, even to this unsatisfactory family, is complete. The world outside is an even worse prospect.

Oshima tells this odd, slightly eccentric tale which might almost have sprung from Dickens completely without sentimentality and secures from the boy the kind of totally natural performance that makes us weep. He seems a very normal child in abnormal circumstances, indulging in science-fiction fantasies and longing for a hero to believe in.

The portrait of Japan Oshima paints is very different from the one Westerners might expect. And his main thrust is that, in such a society, rushing towards the economic miracle that was later to be so rudely interrupted, there remain large numbers of people who will always be left behind. In these circumstances, it is perhaps not so surprising that the family is not even aware that it is doing wrong. It is simply trying to survive.

Some of Oshima's films, which all come from the left, even if he began to hate the leaders of the Communist Party he initially sympathised with, seem to be influenced by either Godard or Buñuel, as well as by a deep suspicion of Japanese traditions. But *Boy* is more like a Truffaut film if it is to be compared with any European work. Its telling, comparatively straightforward narrative is linked to a warmth of expression that Oshima has seldom emulated since.

MADAME DE...

Directed by Max Ophuls
With Danielle Darrieux, Vittorio De Sica, Charles Boyer
France/Italy, 1953, 102 minutes

There is usually a film by the great Max Ophuls in my best ten of all time, let alone the best hundred. It is not *La Ronde*, his most successful film, nor *Lola Montes*, the magnificent last work of a career in film that spanned 25 years and took in Germany, Italy and France as well as Hollywood. That film has been called his *Zauberflote*. My favourite, however, is the film that preceded it – *Madame De...*

The film is one of four he made towards the end of his life in France after leaving Hollywood and such less satisfactory but still impressive melodramas as *Caught* and *Reckless Moment*. And it encapsulates both his dazzling technique and the way that technique serves and ennobles what looks like very slight material.

The story, taken from a novella by Louise de Vilmorin but translated by Ophuls into something more like Pirandello or Anna Karenina, revolves (quite literally) around a pair of earrings. They are given to Madame De... (Danielle Darrieux) by her husband (Charles Boyer). But she sells them to pay her debts, only for her husband to buy them back and give them to his mistress.

The mistress also sells them, and they are bought by a diplomat (Vittorio de Sica) who falls for none other than Madame De... Now her husband discovers the whole secret, and tells the diplomat, who gives her up. Losing the one true love of her life, she dies of a broken heart.

If this isn't intrinsically a novella, I don't know what is. But by the time Ophuls has finished, it seems a great deal more than that.

This is not because the film looks so beautiful or is acted so well, though both these things are true. Darrieux was a warmer, more vulnerable adornment to the French cinema than Catherine Deneuve, and she succeeds in maturing from a flighty young thing into a truly passionate woman as the plot unfolds. I can't remember better performances from De Sica or Boyer either. It's principally due to Ophuls' capacity to turn what could be described as an almost decadent sense of ornamentation into something aware and acutely personal.

It was one of the most highly honed and polished styles in world cinema, with elaborate camera movements, and shimmering and ornate decor that shows us, in this case, an extravagant material world in which the earrings become emblematic of domestic tragedy.

In the famous ball sequence, Ophuls manages to suggest first the gaiety of Madame De...'s dance with her lover, then the deepening of their

love for one another, and finally the impending disaster. At the end of it, a flunkey puts out light after light in the ballroom and, as he throws a cover over a harp, we end in darkness. The pacing is perfect and every element of the film-making process contributes to the whole.

You could say, of course, that *Madame De...*, like the equally fine *Lola Montes* and *Letter from An Unknown Woman*, is a woman's picture, carrying reminders of such Hollywood alumni as Douglas Sirk. And many of Ophuls's movies were centred on women. But if that means sentimental, or at least equipped with a penchant for mythologising womanhood, it would not be wholly true. If it means showing us the difficulties women have in a male-dominated society, it would be pretty accurate.

What once prevented critics treating Ophuls seriously was, in fact, the splendour of his film-making. Somehow that meant he was not wholly to be trusted, as if irony and a lightness of touch simply meant stylish flippancy. Now, however, we see him as he is – a film-maker whose admirers included such diverse artists as Genet, Truffaut, Rossellini and Preston Sturges.

And if Robert Altman is often credited with sound-tracks within which much more is heard than simply the dialogue of the actors leading the scene, then those who give that credit can't have seen Ophuls's films, which, much to the annoyance of his sound engineers, use the same tactic. He sometimes said he liked to film life indirectly 'by ricochet'. Ophuls died of rheumatic heart disease in 1957. He was only fifty-five and had made 21 films. The themes of most of them were the same – the transitory nature of pleasure and the illusory nature of happiness. His method was simple, even though his technique was not. He once said: 'Details, details, details! The most insignificant, the most unobtrusive among them are often the most evocative, characteristic and even decisive. Exact details, an artful little nothing, make art.'

BLUE VELVET

Directed by David Lynch
With Kyle MacLachlan, Isabella Rossellini, Dennis Hopper
USA, 1986, 120 minutes

Those who celebrated the success of Sam Mendes' admittedly accomplished *American Beauty* as a scorching exposure of American suburbia might benefit from taking another look at David Lynch's *Blue Velvet*, a much more radical and disturbing fable on the same subject. It is, without doubt, one of the seminal films of the eighties, from which sprang a good many inferior imitations. I wouldn't say the more mainstream Mendes film was that. But it would have looked more original had the Lynch film never been made.

Lynch is not a director everyone likes, except when it comes to *The Straight Story*, his latest and most orthodox film, and *The Elephant Man*, an earlier essay in comparatively straight narrative. Both these were excellent films, but the power and originality of *Eraserhead*, *Blue Velvet* and possibly the first *Twin Peaks* was what makes his place in cinema history secure.

Blue Velvet, like *American Beauty* and Todd Solontz's extraordinary *Happiness*, places sex at the base of domestic trauma. So much so, in fact, that what he delivered to his audiences without compromise was considered reprehensible by many. This is because it was taken literally. But as Isabella Rossellini, who plays the masochistic nightclub singer beaten up by Dennis Hopper's kidnapper, has said, Lynch's films are not so much psychological studies of character as surreal impressions – 'more of a sensation than a story'.

The film has such raw and often painful energy that you either love or hate it. Its different levels are what puzzle people. On the one hand we have a portrait of small-town Lumberton suffused with a dead-pan irony that encourages us to think the film is some sort of satire. On the other we have what lies behind this often ludicrous facade, which is sex, passion and so many worms in the bud that the film also qualifies as a horror story.

When college student Kyle MacLachlan finds a severed ear in a field, and he and his girl (Laura Dern) try to solve the mystery, the film takes an abrupt turn leftwards. The trail leads to the nightclub singer in whose flat, hidden in a closet, the student first watches Hopper's sado-masochistic tryst and is then horrified when she discovers him after Hopper has left and forces him to submit to similar treatment. This is the disturbing core of the film. And Rossellini's selfless performance, during which she has to submit to a myriad of indignities, is the equal of Lynch's curious imagination.

If this caused the outrage at the time, it was the director's capacity to change tack and revert to an irony that almost amounts to parody that disturbed audiences still further. Was this simply a joke in very bad taste? Actually, it wasn't. It was a recognition that behind even the most banal of people and circumstances lie some pretty peculiar truths. 'Are you a detective or a pervert?' asks Dern of her boyfriend at one point. The answer is a bit of both, and maybe, Lynch suggests, that goes for all of us.

The film is one of the most uncomfortable I have seen, and by no means flawless. For instance, Hopper's character is never fully explained, and there are passages of psychotic excess that don't make too much sense. But the power of the whole is undeniable, distinctively augmented by Angelo Badalamenti's music.

Perhaps the best summation of it comes from Lynch himself, quoted in Chris Rodley's *Lynch on Lynch*: 'Well, film is really voyeurism. You sit there in the safety of the theatre, and seeing is such a powerful thing. And we want to see secret things, we really want to see them. New things. It drives you nuts, you know! And the more new and secret they are, the more you want to see them.'

A NIGHT AT THE OPERA

Directed by Sam Wood
With the Marx Brothers
USA, 1936, 93 minutes

When I first went to see the Marx Brothers I wasn't overly enamoured. Actually I preferred Laurel and Hardy, or even Abbott and Costello. I still prefer Laurel and Hardy, but have to admit a grave mistake when comparing Abbott and Costello to Groucho, Chico and Harpo. Part of the

trouble was that every time I went to see a Marx Brothers epic, the audience laughed so much that I couldn't hear more than a quarter of the verbal gags. At that time, just after the Second World War, they were so popular amongst the intelligentsia they so often mocked that you almost took against them.

I now know better. And the only question is whether one goes for the more anarchic if more awkward Paramount movies like *Monkey Business* and *Duck Soup*, certain masterpieces of anti-bourgeois insanity, or the smoother, more music-oriented MGM films like *A Night at the Opera* and *A Day at the Races*. Most aficionados prefer the Paramount films, which hardly enhanced but seldom interfered with their comedy, and caused one American critic to write that the Marx Brothers had never been in a picture as wonderful as they were.

But *A Night at the Opera* is marginally my choice, because it was the film that changed all that, with producer Irving Thalberg fulfilling his promise to make 'a big-time act using small-time material' into big-time all the way. 'Don't worry about a thing,' Thalberg said to Harpo, 'You get me the laughs and I'll get you the story'.

They did and he did, first insisting that they took the show out on the road as a stage attraction in order to hone it to perfection. This was why the famous state-room scene, in which the brothers and several passengers pack into one small ship's bedroom, has become a classic. Apparently no one laughed until it had been embellished by the brothers on the stage with a series of ad-libs that eventually became part of the script.

The film has several other amazing sequences – notably the contract-tearing farrago between Groucho and Chico and the crazy finale in which Harpo does a Tarzan act on the flyropes perfectly in tune with Verdi's music. But its level of invention is consistently high from the moment Harpo fences with the starchy opera-house conductor, misleading the orchestra into turning the overture to *Il Trovatore* into a rousing rendition of 'Take Me Out to the Ball Game', as Groucho paces the stalls with cigar selling peanuts.

One has to say that, despite the sentimental songs from Allan Jones and Kitty Carlisle, who also provide the unlikely romance, the assaults on grand opera are at least as iconoclastic as anything the dadaists committed to the screen earlier. Buñuel, for one, loved them. And considering this was an MGM super-production, it seems a miracle that Thalberg permitted it to be sabotaged so thoroughly. His successors did not, and the brothers found themselves adrift in MGM movies that did them scant justice.

Of course you could say that the brothers' humour was often cruel and defiantly misogynistic, and by all accounts they weren't all that pleasant to deal with. But they laid the ground for the Pythons and others to till and their nose-thumbing at proprieties shows Jewish–American humour at its most original. Who else could have managed the scene when Harpo climbs through a porthole into the cabin of a liner where three bearded men are sleeping? He picks up a pair of scissors with his eyes alight, lifts a beard and a butterfly flutters out. What is this if it isn't surreal?

THE BATTLE OF ALGIERS

Directed by Gillo Pontecorvo
With Jean Martin, Yacef Saadi
Italy/Algeria, 1965, 136 minutes

Few fictional films look more like documentary than Gillo Pontecorvo's *The Battle of Algiers*, and very few indeed, which have this kind of socio-political structure and which recount old, half-forgotten conflicts, have achieved such lasting fame. Certainly, Pontecorvo himself never managed to repeat the trick, though *Queimada!*, for which he hired Marlon Brando to play the British agent sent to the Caribbean to stir up rebellion againt the Portuguese, was at least a partial success three years later.

The Battle of Algiers, however, remains the basis of Pontecorvo's fame – a model of how, without prejudice or compromise, a film-maker can illuminate history and, in hindsight, tell us how we repeat the same mistakes again and again. This study of the Algerian guerilla struggle against the French colonialists in the fifties ought, in fact, to be looked at not just as pure cinema but as a terrible warning to those who seek by force to stamp out independence movements.

We know, of course, that Algeria was eventually liberated from the French. But Pontecorvo relegates that to an epilogue. He concentrates instead on the years between 1954 and 1957 when the FLN freedom fighters regrouped and expanded into the Casbah, only to face a systematic attempt by French paratroopers to wipe them out. What his highly dramatic film is about is the organisation of a guerilla movement and the methods used to decimate it by the colonial power.

Its stance is as fair as any such film could be, despite the fact that Pontecorvo was a member of the Italian Communist Party at the time and thus tacitly on the side of the independence movement. There is, though, no caricature and no glamorisation of one side or the other. Just a feeling of palpable horror at what happened through some of the most urgent images imaginable, orchestrated by Ennio Morricone's dramatic but never melodramatic score. He sees the colonialists as victims of their own system, and the rebels as taking on some of the excesses used against them.

I remember one scene in particular. It has a group of ordinary people, French and Algerian, having coffee and conversation near the Casbah, and then a rebel bomb exploding among them. The shock of this sequence is even worse than the scenes of French torture. These are seen as at least partially justified – provided you agree with the cause the perpetrators espouse.

The film is preceded by a message from the film-maker stating that 'not one foot' of newsreel footage was used, but Marcello Gatti's grainy, black-and-white camerawork in the actual locations of the struggle, and the pioneering hand-held camerawork used for the crowd scenes, looks as if events are being recorded as they occur. The mixture of amateurs and professionals in the cast works admirably too.

In a way this is all cheating, and Pontecorvo once received as much criticism as praise. The left wanted more commitment to the rebel cause. The right objected that there was too much objectivity. Now, however, *The Battle of Algiers* is regarded as the precursor of films like Rosi's *Salvatore Guiliano* and Costa-Gavras's *Z* – a film which allows its viewers to re-examine their own attitudes towards their times, while making clear that no one can prevent the march of history in certain almost preordained forms.

The film, which won the Golden Lion at the Venice Festival, was then banned in France for some time, and the torture scenes cut from versions distributed in Britain and America. It can now be seen whole and is frequently shown as a model to those who wish to make either fiction or docudrama.

TRASH

Directed by Paul Morrissey
With Holly Woodlawn, Joe Dallesandro
USA, 1970, 103 minutes

A former British Censor once said to me of Paul Morrissey's *Trash*: 'It's all very well you middle-class people trotting along to see such films at the ICA or somewhere arty like that. But what do you suppose might happen if *Trash* were presented to a working-class audience in Manchester?' Which is rather like asking, as Sir Reginald Manningham-Buller, nick-named Bullingham Manner, did during the *Lady Chatterley's Lover* trial, whether you'd like your servants to read the book.

The answer, of course, is that the middle classes did indeed lap up this story of a down-and-out junkie and his girl living on New York's Lower East Side, while the Manchester audience was never given the chance, though it might well have thrown its popcorn at the screen and left after 40 minutes or so. But the fact that films like *Trash* and *Flesh* were once seen as dangerous now seems to pass all understanding.

There are two views of *Heat* and this seminal film from the early seventies. One is that Morrissey is to be praised for imposing an even vaguely coherent story and fleshed out character onto this Warholian epic. And that its 'liberating frankness', which so worried the Censor, actually masked an almost puritan and certainly right-wing morality. The other is that Morrissey should be censured, if not censored, for ruining the formal integrity of something like *Chelsea Girls* with conventionally authored and plotted films that were a mixture of prurience and condescension.

In fact, Morrissey certainly took a strict attitude towards drug-taking. He considered his characters worse than the Bowery winos, and the film a counterattack against the romanticising of drug use in *Easy Rider*. 'The basic idea is that drug people are trash. There's no difference between a person using drugs and a piece of refuse.' The film itself, however, was more compassionate, suggesting that its two leading characters were capable of salvaging something of their ruined lives through tenderness and loyalty.

Joe (Dallesandro) and Holly (Woodlawn, a transvestite who told Morrissey she was a Warhol superstar despite never having met him) live in a basement apartment they furnish with trash from the street. His heroin addiction has rendered him impotent, and the plot concerns Holly's abortive efforts to save him from himself, and the oddities they meet on the way. The uptown people who pass through their orbit include a rich girl who wants LSD, a topless dancer and a newly wed couple fascinated by the lurid.

Although it is clear that most of the women, and some of the men, including probably the director, want Joe's body – and the film is in one sense a kind of paean to it – it is Woodlawn who dominates *Trash*, with Morrissey accepting totally that he/she is a woman. She has said that she wanted to seem ridiculous and make people laugh, but also that the watcher should feel something for a woman who craves some sort of normality in her life. It is a performance that manages both, even in the notorious sequence where she masturbates with a beer bottle, gripping the impotent Joe's hand as she does so.

If the film is primitively made, with Morrissey's static tripod camera augmented only by documentary inserts of street life, it isn't just an exploitative piece of sexual and social exotica. It has a kind of slightly twisted heart and mind behind it. Whether you think Morrissey betrayed Warhol or not, Morrissey's view of his mentor was probably right.

He said: 'Andy wasn't capable of any complicated thoughts or ideas. Ideas need a verb and a noun, a subject. Andy spoke in a kind of stumbling staccato. You had to finish sentences for him. So Andy operated through people who could do things for him. He wished things into happening, things he himself couldn't do. In that respect he was like Louis B. Mayer at MGM.'

ANDREI ROUBLEV

Directed by Andrei Tarkovsky
With Anatoly Solonitsyn, Ivan Lapikov
USSR, 1966, 185 minutes

'In a good period I could have been a millionaire. Making two films a year from 1960 on when I could have made 20... Fat chance with our idiots' – from Tarkovsky's *Diaries*, 1970.

In fact, Tarkovsky, the greatest, and most imitated, director Russia has produced over the last 50 years, ended up making seven full-length films between 1962, when *Ivan's Childhood* burst upon the world, and 1986, when *The Sacrifice* was completed as he found himself stricken with cancer. Two of these films were made outside Russia, where the authorities deeply suspected his motives and were unwilling to accord him state funds.

In defence of the authorities (who often were indeed idiots and placemen), Tarkovsky was a difficult man to please. As an artist he felt entitled to be. I remember visiting the location set of *The Sacrifice* on the Swedish island of Faroe, sometimes known as Bergman's Island. It was bitterly cold, and since a night scene was called for, the cast, including the British actress Susan Fleetwood, waited for Tarkovsky shivering in flimsy night attire. He was half an hour late and, according to a production assistant, had spent much of that time staring at himself in the mirror, adjusting and readjusting his scarf and fur hat.

'If he wasn't such a damned good director,' Fleetwood said, 'I'd have left long ago'.

But, of course, he was a damned fine director – a metaphorical looking-glass, as one critic has said, that provides man with a reflection of himself. Perhaps his most Russian film, and oddly enough the film that has always been the most appreciated in the West, was *Andrei Roublev*, Tarkovsky's second, made when he was thirty-four. It is epic in scale and scope (three hours long and nothing less than his version of *The Birth of a Nation*, being a commentary on the physical and spiritual foundations of Russia itself).

Roublev was not a fictional character but an icon painter and monk who lived and worked on the cusp of the thirteenth and fourteenth centuries, trained by the even more celebrated Theophanes the Greek. Not much is known about him, though his work is now better appreciated, thanks to the film. And what Tarkovsky attempted was to paint a convincing portrait of the time, as much through psychological truth as ethnographic accuracy. The unaltering landscape of Russia did the rest.

'Our Russia – it has to endure everything,' says Roublev at one point to the spectre of Theophanes, to which his Old Testament master replies presciently that it probably always will. The film begins with a peasant launching himself in a balloon from atop a cathedral across the landscape of medieval Russia, and ends with a superb montage of Roublev's surviving icons. In between, Roublev witnesses the often horrific sufferings of a divided Russia, split between feuding princelings and Tartar invaders.

There are eight episodes in all, the most notable being the story of a young boy who, to save his life, pretends he can cast a giant bell and succeeds in doing so through blind faith – a feat which inspires Roublev to paint again.

The film is as much about the role of the artist in society as it is about the emergence of the Russian nation. Roublev can only give expression to his art by sharing the sufferings of the age in which he lives. Passivity is not an option. All Tarkovsky's films say this in one way or another, and

it is their intensely spiritual preoccupations, and their poetic formulation of them on the screen, that sets them apart.

They intend to be as timeless as the music of Taverner, but in my opinion with considerably greater strength. You can object to Tarkovsky's 'alternative reality' as Messianic and sometimes fundamentalist. It is difficult, however, to mock the impact of his films. He was, in a way, a latterday Roublev.

WITCHFINDER GENERAL

Directed by Michael Reeves
With Vincent Price, Ian Ogilvy
UK, 1968, 87 minutes

If the purpose of this series is, at least in part, to remind people of extraordinary films they may have forgotten, or even never seen, then *Witchfinder General* (retitled *The Conqueror Worm* in America) qualifies better than most. Michael Reeves, its British director, killed himself at the age of twenty-five. Had he had a full career, we would certainly know him better. This was the last of his three films, made at the age of only twenty-three, and it is one of the most compulsively watchable ever made in Britain.

Yet it looks, in certain ways, like a strange kind of Hammer horror, using the history of Cromwellian times to tell a story that makes the flesh creep. That, no doubt, is what Tigon, its producers, hoped. But it is considerably more than exploitation.

Filmed on a very modest budget in the Norfolk and Suffolk countryside, its star is Vincent Price, an actor often on the edge of parodying himself but, under a good director, able to drop his slightly camp mannerisms and produce something special. He plays Matthew Hopkins, an infamous and cruel lawyer turned witch-hunter, culled from history, who sets about travelling the countryside and rooting out those opposed to the revolution.

Taken from a well researched if portentous novel by Roland Bassett, the film keeps much of the book's Freudian sexual undertones but adds to its strange erotic charge a study of violent and superstitious times that is baroque, disturbing and at times even poetic.

The tone is set with the horrific execution of a woman accused of witchcraft. After being dragged screaming across a windy plain, she is hanged from a gibbet on a desolate hill, with a priest mouthing litanies beside her. At once, Reeves's use of the landscape and firm hold on drama is apparent. This is a frightening sequence which underlines the terror of the times and the deeply ingrained evil of religious fanatacism.

The real victim of the film, however, is a soldier who fought bravely for Cromwell and now wishes to settle down with his wife in the countryside. The witchfinder accuses his wife, and in the end traps the soldier and tortures her in front of him. Finally breaking the chains that bind him, he hacks her tormentor to pieces.

If this sounds like your average horror movie, it takes no account of the tension Reeves creates throughout, how he persuades some less than wonderful actors to feel their parts, how he contrasts the evil of the times with the quiet, bare countryside and how he makes the period come alive with a few imaginative brush-strokes. Johnny Coquillon was the innovative cinematographer.

Reeves's two other films were less notable, though promising much. One, *La Sorella di Satana* (1965), made very cheaply in Italy, where he was given four days of the horror icon Barbara Steele's time, still manages to achieve something to compare with masters such as Mario Bava. The other was *The Sorcerers* (1967), made in England with Boris Karloff, which some think rivals the intelligence of Michael Powell's *Peeping Tom*. Few, however, have seen either.

All three films were commercially oriented, but *Witchfinder General* transcends its genre with the sheer panache of its making within a period when Polanski made *Repulsion, Dance of the Vampires* and *Rosemary's Baby* and Bergman *The Hour of the Wolf*. That the film stands up well against such opposition, and that of the best of Hammer, reflects on the standing of its director. He was much more than simply promising, and deserves to be remembered.

LES ENFANTS DU PARADIS

Directed by Marcel Carné
With Arletty, Jean-Louis Barrault, Pierre Brasseur
France, 1945, 188 minutes

'What a strange and sad fate – to be universally acclaimed as the director of several of the finest films ever made, and to go on making films to which no one pays any attention.' So wrote Richard Roud, my predecessor as *Guardian* critic, of Marcel Carné, the maker of *Les Enfants du Paradis*, Europe's answer in the affections of almost everybody to hugely popular Hollywood films like *Casablanca* and *Gone with the Wind*.

Roud added shrewdly that *Les Enfants* was to the French cinema of the thirties what *Gone with the Wind* was to the American cinema of the time: a summing up, a fully realised expression of the period, and also the death-knell for a certain kind of cinema some people wish we still had now. And he counteracts the view that Carné was never a great director, that it was thanks to the ideas and scripts of his partner Jacques Prevert that Carné achieved his prominence, by pointing out that Prevert was as responsible as Carné for the first of the many post-war disasters like *Les Portes de la Nuit* and *La Marie du Port*.

The fact is that Carné and Prevert formed a partnership as productive as any in the history of the cinema until they had nothing more to say, largely because times had changed. *Les Enfants* was its apogee, inspired by the popular theatre of the nineteenth century but translated into an epic cinematic romance that will probably never be equalled for both substance and style.

Three of its extraordinary gallery of characters, all of them given due weight, are based on historical figures – the pantomime artist Debureau, the romantic actor Frederic Lemaitre and the criminal Lacenaire. Each falls in love with, and is briefly loved by, Garance, a beautiful actress who leaves them only when her freedom is threatened by their attempts to possess her. They meet in the neighbourhood of the Théatre Funambules

in Paris, sometimes called the Boulevard du Crime, which was reconstructed at great cost, amazingly enough when the Nazis occupied Paris, with sets that stretched over a quarter of a mile.

Actually the Germans encouraged the production, which caused it to be either sabotaged or halted when various members of the cast could not be found. Some of them, working for the French underground, had their scenes shot secretly. And Carné and Prevert hid key reels from the occupiers, hoping that by the time the film was finished Paris would be liberated.

If the film is to be understood fully, the contemporary watcher should be reminded that 'paradis' is the colloquial name for the theatre's gallery, where the 'real' people watched and vociferously commented upon their entertainments, and to whom the actors pitched their performances. You could say the film is about freedom, symbolised by the sophisticated Garance. But it is as much about our reactions to what is going on, and the actors' reactions to them. We, in this case, are the gallery.

Certainly the performances are marvellous, and superbly directed by Carné too, easily transcending Prevert's sometimes precious though undeniably skilful text. They are led by Arletty as Garance, an actress whose beauty and grace was matchless (she had posed for Braque and Matisse) and whose capacity to suggest not only the spirit of popular theatre, but also the 'new woman' who needed and deserved her liberty, made her every moment vivid. Curiously, she was jailed as a collaborator when *Les Enfants* opened, largely because she had had an affair with a Luftwaffe officer during the war.

But if Arletty is unforgettable, Barrault as the pantomine artist (which he was in life), Brasseur as the romantic Lemaitre and Marcel Herrand as the criminal are not far behind, centring the huge canvas of the film, which was much more than a costume drama, securely for its three-hour duration. Cinema and poetry are the same thing, Prevert said in an interview before the film's first showing. Not always, alas. But it's surely true here.

MEMORIES OF UNDERDEVELOPMENT

Directed by Tomás Gutiérrez Alea
With Sergio Corrieri, Daisy Granados
Cuba, 1968, 104 minutes

Of all the dozens of films produced in Cuba through Castro's insistence on the importance of the cinema, *Memories of Underdevelopment* is the most sophisticated. So much so, in fact, that those opposed to the revolution tend to call it a magnificent and unrepeatable fluke, produced as it was by a film institute that was virtually a Marxist ministry. Those in favour cherish it as a landmark that almost totally avoids the usual radical cliches.

Not surprisingly under the circumstances, it became the film through which Europe and America first judged what was happening in Cuba at ground level.

The director was Tomás Gutiérrez Alea, a middle-class university-educated Cuban who went along with the revolution despite some of the doubts about emerging bureaucratisation the equally bourgeois protagonist of his film evinces. He is Sergio, a wealthy man who decides to stay behind when his family leaves for the States. The time is 1961, and the film is placed between the exodus from Cuba after the disastrous Bay of Pigs invasion and the defensive preparations for the missile crisis of the following year.

Sergio's thoughts and experiences as a member of the educated elite as he is confronted by the new Cuban reality form the nub of the film. He is fundamentally an alienated outsider, scornful of his bourgeois family and friends, but also of the naivete of those who believe that everything can suddenly be changed for the better. He continues to live as a rent-collecting property owner and, in his private life, chases women with an almost neurotic fervour.

He is, in fact, the sort of man with whom we can easily identify from any experience of European films and literature. The difference is that he is placed in exceptional circumstances and finds it difficult to understand them. *Memories* is one of the best films ever made about the sceptical individual's place in the march of revolutionary history.

None of this would have been enough if Alea hadn't constructed his film so richly, and in excitingly cinematic rather than literary terms. Documentary and semi-documentary footage is presented as Sergio would have seen it, and the fictional story that goes along with it is very European in its narrative style. There are even clips from a porno film included – there were many made in Cuba during Batista's regime – and Alea himself and the author of the original novel comment on what is going on in Sergio's mind.

As one admiring critic has said, 'The film insists that what we see is a function of how we believe, and that how we believe is what our history has made of us'.

Memories was Alea's fifth film, and probably his most famous, though at least three others received international attention. *Death of a Bureaucrat* was an ironic satire on the way revolutions stiffen into deadly bureaucracies; *The Last Supper* showed how the black slaves of Cuba in the plantation era were reconciled by religion to a life of bondage, and *Strawberry and Chocolate* was a brave and popular film which, despite Castro's disdain for homosexuality, dared to have a stolid party cadre befriended and changed by a gay man.

Alea was clearly no ordinary product of the revolutionary cinema. He died recently of cancer and was honoured by a government he supported but often quietly criticised, and even more by the ordinary Cubans who flocked to his films.

THE BIRTH OF A NATION

Directed by D.W. Griffith
With Henry B. Walthall, Miriam Cooper, Mae Marsh, Lillian Gish
USA, 1915, 134 minutes

According to Kevin Brownlow, D.W. Griffith was 'the only director in America creative enough to be called a genius'. To Charles Higham he was the founding father of Hollywood, who 'imported a provincialism, a bourgeois Philistinism from which it has never escaped'. According to James Agee, *The Birth of a Nation* is 'equal to Brady's photographs, Lincoln's speeches, and Whitman's war poems'. To John Simon, the film is 'morally objectionable, and artistically and intellectually insufficient'.

This barrage of conflicting views has never prevented Griffith being regarded as a great, ground-breaking director, nor *The Birth of a Nation* as a key film in the evolution of the medium. Yet you can't possibly look at it now without understanding the accusations of racism, or the moral embarrassment of those critics who used to include it in their lists of the ten best films ever made.

Griffith's immediate source was *The Clansman*, a play based by Thomas Dixon Jr on two turn-of-the-century novels which represented the South as some kind of Arcadia from which all the best features of American life had sprung. But this stupendously nostalgic and wish-fulfilling work was whittled down by the director (who himself came from the South) into a paean to the female-oriented values of the family, and to a society where everyone, including black slaves, seem to know their place. It was not for nothing that the central image of *Intolerance*, his other great masterwork, was a mother rocking her cradle.

The Civil War and its aftermath gave Griffith the opportunity to make the South as a whole into an heroic family, but it also allowed him to emphasise, through the climactic rescue scene where Southerners and Northerners fight side by side – and the earlier cross-barrier love affairs of the protagonists – that all Americans were part of the same clan. Unfortunately he also emphasised, in that part of the film that corresponded most closely with Dixon's play, the danger that black America, migrating en masse from the South, would prove a threat to everything he held dear.

Under the circumstances, how can such a film possibly be considered great? There are three good reasons. The first is that the film wasn't just ground-breaking in its technique. It was the way that technique was applied to dramatise the story that is impressive – to take one example, the length of each shot was designed so as to influence our emotional response, with dramatic scenes cut faster. There are many other such totally new concepts for a large-scale feature film. And, astonishingly, Griffith did all this, using one camera and two lenses, in a mere nine weeks.

The second reason for its greatness is that the film marked, in America at least, the effective birth of a cinema that wasn't just mere entertainment but a fully-fledged art form that could still be appreciated by the masses. The third is that the director's reliance on and support for his actors, and particularly his actresses, which was not so much concerned with making them into luminous stars as real people capable, like the great Lillian Gish, of interpreting their parts with a proper honesty.

Unlike the even more epic *Intolerance*, which is glorious and dull in turn, *The Birth of a Nation* holds the watcher as in a vice because it shows such ingenuity in integrating a very intimate story within the framework of so large an historical canvass. However much you object to its actual interpretation of history, you have to admit this. You also have to admit that the quasi-Victorian Griffith was in so many respects way ahead of his time, even if his philosophy and mind-set could often be said to be behind it. *The Birth of a Nation* thus remains a great film even if its stature is tarnished.

THRONE OF BLOOD

Directed by Akira Kurosawa
With Toshiro Mifune, Isuzu Yamada
Japan, 1957, 105 minutes

It is generally easier to decide which directors to include in any top hundred than which film would best represent them. Akira Kurosawa, who died recently, looks likely to remain by far the most familiar Japanese director in the world at large, whereas directors as great as him, or even greater, like Naruse, Ozu and Mizoguchi, are only known by cineasts.

But which film should one choose to typify his art? Most would say either *The Seven Samurai*, the epic which inspired John Sturges's popular but lesser *The Magnificent Seven*, *Rashomon*, the film which so amazed the West at the Venice Festival of 1951 with its versions of a murder as described by different witnesses, or *Living*, the elegiac story of a old civil servant who, dying of cancer, tries to find a meaning to his life by building a children's playground in a slum area.

Each of these is a masterwork, and there are others. But my choice remains 1957's *Throne of Blood*, known also as *Cobweb Castle*, an adaptation

of Shakespeare's *Macbeth* which turns the Scottish play into a ravishingly visual exploration of the warrior traditions of Japanese myth. It was, for what it is worth, T. S. Eliot's favourite film.

The drama is presented with stark economy, its words subservient to the slow exposition of its plot, and its characterisation admittedly less subtle than Shakespeare's. But I doubt whether the bard would have turned in his grave. Kurosawa's parallel eloquence matches Shakespeare's so completely that it even outshines that of Verdi's musical version.

Right at the beginning we watch Kurosawa's Macbeth (here called Washuzi and interpreted by Toshiro Mifune, his favourite leading man) and his friend Miki riding through the misty, rain-soaked pine forests before his meeting with the witch (the director allows us only one).

When they return, we are not sure at first where we are, even as watchers. The pair ride 12 times towards the camera before turning away, as if inhibited by some unseen obstacle. Finally they reach the plain, from which they see the warlord's castle. It is a daring coup the like of which I have never seen before or since, and as perfect a series of tracking shots as have ever been devised.

But the technique doesn't draw attention to itself, except in dramatic terms, and nor does it do so when Washuzi watches as Cobweb Forest (Birnam Wood) looms nearer and nearer to the Castle or when, at the end, wooden arrows from the avenging army virtually crucify him again and again.

The film alternates a deathly stillness with crescendos of violent action, and gains from its relationship not just to the bones of Shakespeare but to the tenets of Noh drama. The mask-like white face of Asaji (Lady Macbeth) seems to make her into a ghost long before she is driven into madness, while the panic of Miki's horse before the off-screen murder of his master, the sudden invasion of the throne room by a flock of birds and the slow funeral procession advancing on the castle gates look like prophecies of the Macbeths' inevitable doom.

Kurosawa has been both criticised in some quarters and praised in others for being the most Western and thus comprehensible of Japanese directors. The criticism is that his work is somehow not properly Japanese. And it is certainly true that the Japanese at one time rejected it, accusing Kurosawa of being too much in thrall to outworn traditions of the past.

The criticism, and his abortive efforts to continue working, caused him to attempt suicide in 1971. In the end he was able to continue with the help of Steven Spielberg, George Lucas and others who saw in him a kind of Eastern David Lean.

Throne of Blood, more than most of his many films, shows that though, like Satyajit Ray, he digested many Western influences – including training as a painter at a Western art school, and an abiding admiration for John Ford – he was as much a product of his own culture as Mizoguchi (whom he acknowledged as his master).

As a piece of cinema, however, *Throne of Blood* defeats catagorisation. It remains a landmark of visual strength, permeated by a particularly Japanese sensibility, and also what is quite possibly the finest Shakespearean adaptation ever committed to the screen.

THE ENIGMA OF KASPAR HAUSER

Written and directed by Werner Herzog
With Bruno S
Germany, 1974, 109 minutes

There is no more entertaining film than Werner Herzog's documentary about his madcap relationship with Klaus Kinski, the dangerously eccentric actor who appeared for him so notably as the conquistador in

Aguirre, Wrath of God. But in Herzog's case truth is often stranger than fiction, so it isn't surprising that most of his films proclaim that loud and clear.

Perhaps the most famous of his romantic allegories is *The Enigma of Kaspar Hauser* – the story, based on truth, of a foundling who had been kept apart from all human contact before being left one day in 1828 in the middle of Nuremberg city square. He had no language, but a prayer book had been placed in one hand and a letter addressed to the local regimental riding master in the other.

Given shelter and taught to speak, he hardly had a better life. Several attempts were made to kill him and he was finally mortally injured by a stab-wound in the chest some five years later. His origins were never discovered and the hostility towards him never properly explained.

There have been many films about humans being brought up in the wild, from *Tarzan* to *Jungle Boy*, but I've only seen two convincing examples. They are Truffaut's *L'Enfant Sauvage* and *Kaspar Hauser*. In the Truffaut film about the wild child of Aveyron, French rationalism holds sway. A good and patient teacher can save the wild child from himself. In Herzog's film, it is German romanticism, with its respect for the incalculable mysteries of life and its deep suspicion of the 'civilised' world.

Kaspar's release from the shackled confines of his underground prison allows him to see for the first time the beauties of the natural universe. But society's attempt to tame him shows that man, not nature, is the trouble. A sequence shows us a painterly cornfield billowing in the wind, with the music of Olando di Lasso on the sound-track. Superimposed is a quotation from Lenz, the tale of another tragic figure. 'But can you not hear the dreadful screaming all around that people usually call silence?' The implication is that Kaspar somehow can.

Clearly Herzog believes there is something in Kaspar that should not be destroyed by a society that wishes to civilise or classify him, or to use him as a freak or a human pet. In this he is aided by an astonishing performance, if performance it is, by Bruno S, an orphan street-singer with no previous acting record who seems to live the part, almost through experience.

If the film appears more self-conscious than Truffaut's, it also strives for a more haunting physical and metaphysical quality. Kaspar has flickering visions of Sahara nomads, pilgrims in the mist near Croagh Patrick in Ireland and the windswept Caucasus landscape. And Tamino's aria, 'Is this feeling Love?' from *The Magic Flute*, is used to emphasise its moral.

Some consider Herzog a mountebank who exploits marginals like Bruno S, and some call him a genuine visionary. He is probably a bit of both. He once claimed to have walked 500 miles from Munich to see Lotte Eisner, the famous film historian, when she was ill in Paris. But he also went there to supervise the subtitling of one of his films before presenting it at Cannes. Besides, Lotte once said to me: 'Nonsense, I met him off the train'. Whatever, *Kaspar Hauser* is one of the most fascinating of films. At his best, Herzog is like no other film-maker I know.

BURDEN OF DREAMS

Directed by Les Blank
With Werner Herzog, Klaus Kinski, Claudia Cardinale
USA, 1982, 94 minutes

Films about film-making are usually deeply self-conscious, and sometimes deceiving. But there's one at least that succeeds, beyond all expectations, in being better than the movie the making of which it describes. Les Blank's *Burden of Dreams* admittedly had it easier than most. The movie it examined was Werner Herzog's *Fitzcarraldo*, made on location deep in the rainforests of South America, many hundreds of miles away from civilisation. It's a monument to the almost masochistic desire of its already eccentric director to do the impossible impossibly well.

Needless to say, almost everything that could happen to the production happened in spades. It's the true story of an arguably mad Irishman called Fitzgerald's attempt to build an opera house in the Amazon, and to bring Enrico Caruso to sing in it. And since Klaus Kinski, the conquistador of *Aguirre, Wrath of God*, played him when Jason Robards went down with amoebic dysentery, to use the word 'arguably' seems merely diplomatic. Kinski's behaviour would have taxed a saint.

Strangely, however, it wasn't much odder than Fitzgerald's. He had initially hatched a plan to build a railroad across the continent, starting off with the profits he earned from the ice factory he built. His new plan was even more audacious.

Added to everything else, the film had to be moved some 1200 miles to a new location when a border war broke out between the local Indians, and even at the new venue the tribesmen felt provoked enough to become alarmingly hostile. Plane crashes, disease, rain and mud disturbed Herzog's efforts to achieve his *tour de force* in the film – getting a team of natives to pull an old steamship up a steep hillside using only block and tackle, and then roll it down the other side.

All this was meat and drink to Blank, a well known and frequently intrepid ethnographic documentarist from Middle America whose own eccentricity must have seemed mild in comparison to everyone else's. But he doesn't attempt to take the mickey. He just records the scene, including Kinski's tempers, the Indians' suspicious and often threatening behaviour, and Herzog's gradual descent into near-hysteria, talking of the evil spirits who ruled the terrain and clearly regarding the film-makers as interlopers. Blank's film includes the only available record of some of the unused scenes with Robards and Mick Jagger, who left after all the delays for a concert tour, doubtless with some relief. It also shows the actual mechanisms by which Herzog hoped to move the old ship halfway up a mountain. A giant bulldozer augments the block-and-pulley, but proves unequal to the task as the Brazilian engineer in charge of the operation storms off, complaining that it is virtually certain that lives will be lost.

This is warts-and-all stuff, made with sympathy but determined to show us as much of the truth as possible. Part of that truth is that Herzog seemed to identify with Fitzgerald (called Fitzcarraldo by the natives), and certainly his plan to make a film in such a place was almost as crazy as the Irishman's opera house daydream. *Fitzcarraldo*, though full of notable sequences, didn't entirely work, since the production was almost impossible to pull together satisfactorily.

Blank's film, however, does. You don't have to have seen *Fitzcarraldo* to appreciate it. It takes on, as *Time Out* accurately said at the time, a crazy life of its own. Good old Les.

THE THIRD MAN

Directed by Carol Reed
With Joseph Cotten, Orson Welles, Alida Valli
UK, 1949, 104 minutes

Carol Reed, the British director, made films for 40 years, but his golden period was brief. It covered three years in the late forties when he made *Odd Man Out*, *The Fallen Idol* and *The Third Man*. These three films alone put him in the forefront of British directors of the period, and the last-named, his second collaboration with Graham Greene, is probably the best film noir ever made out of Britain. Like all the best of the genre, the film is deeply romantic, despite its surface cynicism, and it's this that has caused it to remain in the public memory for so long.

Set in a crumbling, depressed post-war Vienna, divided into areas by the Allies' occupying forces, it was a city Reed knew well from his wartime experiences and, beautifully shot by Robert Krasker in the kind of atmospheric black-and-white that would have been destroyed by the use of colour, it almost seems another character in the story. It was further distinguished by several performances that remain in the memory, particularly from Orson Welles, who only took the part of Harry Lime to

help finance his *Othello*, and later regretted he had asked for a salary rather than a share of the profits.

Curiously, David O. Selznick, the American co-producer with Alexander Korda, wanted Noel Coward for the part. If he had played it, we would never have had the most famous lines in the film, written by Welles himself – 'In Italy for 30 years under the Borgias, they had warfare, terror, murder and bloodshed. But they produced Michelangelo, Leonardo da Vinci and the Renaissance. In Switzerland, they had brotherly love and they had 500 years of democracy and peace. And what did they produce? The cuckoo clock!'

This somewhat disputatious statement has haunted the Swiss ever since, and the film's insistent zither music by Anton Karas haunts those who see the film for almost as long. Karas was found by Trevor Howard playing outside a restaurant in Vienna, and his music instantly pitched him into celebrity status.

Greene dreamt up the part of the wicked but charming Harry Lime, the old school friend Joseph Cotten's Holly Martins searches for, after finding an envelope on which he had written, some time before: 'I had paid my last farewell to Harry a week ago, when his coffin was lowered into the frozen February ground, so it was with incredulity that I saw him pass by, without a sign of recognition, among the host of strangers in the Strand'.

It was, of course, first a novel and then a screenplay, but it was one of the few Greene adaptations more successful on the screen than on the page. There are at least two extraordinary sequences – the first showdown between Lime and Martins on the slowly revolving Ferris wheel of an almost deserted fairground, and the chase through the sewers of Vienna that ends with Lime's death. Hitchcock could not have accomplished these sequences better, and there is no doubt that Reed owed some sort of debt to him.

Perhaps melodrama is never very far away, and the romance between Martins and the beautiful Alida Valli, once Lime's girl, could be thought to stretch things a bit in the direction of *Casablanca*. But we shouldn't forget the serious core to the film which embodies in the figure of Lime the corruption and exploitation of the post-war years in Central Europe. Lime was, after all, only a precursor of the contemporary drug dealer, a fact which makes the film oddly relevant even today.

Reed was one of the numerous illegitimate children of the famous actor–manager Beerbohm Tree, and became one of those rather patrician directors in which Britain specialised before films like *Room at the Top* made them look more like ace craftsmen than true *auteurs*. *The Third Man*, however, will live in people's affections as long as Lean's *Brief Encounter*, Hitchcock's *Rebecca* or Powell's *A Matter of Life and Death* as a popular film that didn't underestimate its audiences' intelligence.

SALVATORE GIULIANO

Directed by Francesco Rosi
With Pietro Camerata
Italy, 1961, 135 minutes

Francesco Rosi, once called the heavy conscience of the Italian cinema, was born in Naples – a possible reason why most of his films are about corruption. His most famous film, though, was made in Sicily. It is almost certainly the best film about the social and political forces that have shaped that benighted island ever made. It looks almost like a documentary as it traces the career and downfall of Salvatore Giuliano, a bandit who became a legend on the island after his violent death in 1950. Yet the word 'Mafia' is never once mentioned, and Giuliano himself is hardly seen. All the superficial cliches of a well-known genre are thus subverted.

Rosi spoke the voice-over narration himself, at least in the Italian version, and structured the film round the bandit's death. He is seen as a corpse in the first sequence, with a city official reading a detailed description of his death. This gives us no clue to the questions we want answered – a deliberate ploy by Rosi, who is determined that we will think for ourselves as the film progresses. He merely provides evidence, often elliptical. But the result is a fascinating study not only of the tentacles of crime but of a whole way of life.

We are not allowed to be passive spectators, because thereafter we see Giuliano only briefly, with Rosi using flashbacks chronicling his story from the end of World War II. We witness the growth of the separatist movement, an attack on a Communist peasant gathering, a kidnapping, and the way government, separatists, police and army link up at one time or another with the criminal forces they were supposed to oppose.

Using Sicilian non-professionals as actors, and with his camera sweeping over the terrain that concealed Giuliano from his opponents, Rosi builds up a formidable picture of a time and a place that has its roots in neo-realism but is more interested in society itself than in the individual characters people like De Sica examined so sympathetically. Giuliano remains a legend throughout, and the nearest we get to a conventional figure is his murderer, who emerges from the background only as the film reaches its final stretch.

Everything in the film was based on extensive research into the history of the time, as well as the official court records and journalistic accounts. But Rosi makes no attempt to make complete sense of them, since it is virtually impossible to do so. At the end of the film, what Rosi has carefully assembled is not so much the facts as a reading of what lies behind the confused story of Giuliano's life.

Possibly only Gillo Pontecorvo's *Battle of Algiers* managed so brilliantly the summation of a slice of by now half-remembered history, and Rosi never quite achieved the same mastery of tone and atmosphere again. Later he made *Lucky Luciano*, a more conventional Mafia story, and films like *The Mattei Case* and *Illustrious Corpses*, dossiers on power and corruption which relied on a much more ornate style and the brilliance of actors like the great Gian Maria Volonte to sustain their considerable eloquence.

But *Salvatore Giuliano* has never been bettered as an interpretation of history without resort to special pleading. It's as if the film-maker is standing back and providing clues which we have to interpret ourselves. Something Hollywood would never do, and which justifies European cinema as much as any other film of what now looks like a golden period.

XALA

Directed by Ousmane Sembene
With Thierno Leye, Seune Samb, Miriam Niang, Younouss Seye
Senegal, 1974, 106 minutes

'The African is, in general, not mature enough for cinema. Cinematograph conventions disrupt him; psychological nuances escape him; rapid successions of images submerge him.' That ludicrous statement was written by the Belgian authorities in the Congo not so very long ago, and the African cinema has laboured under so many constraints, whether colonial or simply financial, that it is surprising it exists at all.

It does, however, and the man who could be called the father of the African cinema is Ousmane Sembene, born in Senegal in 1923. He has not made many films, but at least two of them, *Xala* and *Ceddo*, deserve to be accounted among the very best. *Xala* is my choice as the African film popular both in the West and in Africa, and thus worthy of its place in the pantheon.

Sembene, a distinguished novelist who wrote in French and lived and worked in France for some time, forsook books for the cinema largely because, as a Marxist, he wanted to reach other than the French and African elite he despised. A scholarship from the Soviet Union in 1961, when he was nearly forty, led him to study with Donskoy and Gerasimov, and *Xala*, in particular, was a direct result of both their teaching and his populist motives.

Xala means sexual impotence, and the film, made in 1974 and culled from his own novel, is a brilliantly funny and ironic satire about the post-colonial era in Senegal which was effective enough to upset the government considerably. It suffered 11 cuts before being permitted release in Dakar.

A new black elite has taken power, and one of its ruling group is the pompous El Hadj Abou Kader, who celebrates by taking a third wife younger than his daughter but can't get it up on the wedding night. His obsession with curing himself leads further and further towards ruin.

No African director has criticised the pretensions and corruption of the continent's rulers more severely than Sembene in *Xala*, nor done it with such quiet hilarity. The ruling classes are contrasted with a group of beggars who represent the people and exact revenge against Kader by first imposing the *xala* spell and then finally stripping him and spitting on him to release it.

Politically, the film is like a bomb exploding the neo-colonialist process as the resplendent African elite receive briefcases stuffed with banknotes from white businessmen in the Chamber of Commerce and are ushered

along a red carpet into Mercs lined up outside after a speech (in French) about 'the African path to socialism'. Kader later has his Merc carefully washed in mineral water.

'You're not a white man,' his future mother-in-law says when he wants to emphasise his modernity by refusing to participate in the traditional ceremony to ensure a successful deflowering of his new bride, 'You're neither fish nor fowl'. And it is the strong depiction of the women that is another quality of *Xala*. 'There can be no progress in Africa if women are left out of account,' Sembene once wrote.

When Kader quarrels violently with his jeans-wearing younger daughter, addressing her in French, she deliberately replies in Wolof. But when finally he gets the point and addresses the Chamber of Commerce in that language instead of French, he is instantly accused of being 'racist, sectarian and reactionary'. The film spares no one – Kader's successor in the Chamber, from which he is eventually expelled, is a common pickpocket – but Sembene still insists that there is a better future for Africa than this.

It is his sense of irony, coupled with his anger, that make his work outstanding and perhaps easier to understand than many African films. Kader is a hoot until you realise how much power he and his kind wield, and the complicity of Europeans in that process.

Of Sembene's other films, *The Money Order* (*Mandabi*), made in 1968 and about the trials of a local trying to cash a cheque sent to him from

France, was the first truly African feature, and *Ceddo*, made in 1977, which looks at Africa's chequered historical past, remains perhaps the most sophisticated. But *Xala*, made for ordinary Africans and seen by them en masse, is Sembene's single most successful critique of his own society.

RAGING BULL

Directed by Martin Scorsese
With Robert De Niro, Cathy Moriarty, Joe Pesci
USA, 1980, 129 minutes

Michael Powell once said of Martin Scorsese: 'He breakfasts on images'. But it still seems surprising that, while editing *Raging Bull*, Scorsese would watch Powell's ballet film *Tales of Hoffman* over and over again 'because of the movement in it'. *Raging Bull* is now considered Scorsese's most perfect film and one of the few American masterworks of the last 20 years. Boxing and ballet clearly have some parallels.

Not everyone thought so at the time. Pauline Kael described De Niro's portrait of boxer Jake La Motta as 'a swollen puppet with only bits and pieces of a character inside' and described the film itself as tabloid grand opera. And though the film got Oscars for its editing (Thelma Schoonmaker, Powell's widow) and for De Niro, Scorsese's nomination as director was unsuccessful. Robert Redford won for the decent but hardly brilliant first feature *Ordinary People*.

Where Kael was undoubtedly right was in her opinion that the film was as much a biography of the genre of boxing movies as about the rise and fall of a particular fighter. Films like *Body and Soul*, *The Set-Up* and *Golden Boy* are recalled with slow motion, rapid cutting and sweeping camera movements. What was new was the emotional and psychological intensity of a time (the forties and fifties), a place (mostly New York, Scorsese's homeground) and a person (a champion fighter who in the end loses everything, largely through jealousy).

When describing La Motta – the man who let himself be hit in order to exhaust his opponents' strength – Scorsese cited St Thomas Aquinas, who observed that animals served God better than man because they lived their natures so purely, without guilt. But at the end of the film, in which he has allowed his almost primeval brutality to extend from the ring into the lives of his wife and brother, he lets La Motta shout in his Miami jail cell: 'I am not an animal!' and begin his redemption by embracing his brother.

It is a typical Scorsese moment, since in almost all his films there is someone who eventually recognises his own soul. His Catholic antecedents are never very far away, nor is the thought that the destructive instincts of man are capable of atonement.

Yet Paul Schrader, who wrote the first screenplay, loosely culled from La Motta's own ghosted book, has said that *Raging Bull* was not a film either Scorsese or he wanted to make. De Niro talked Scorsese into it and then the two of them talked him into it. It is by now common knowledge that De Niro was obsessed with the part and not only spent ten weeks perfecting the fight scenes but took two breaks away from the shoot to eat his way around Italy and France in order to gain weight for the second half of the film.

He went from his usual 145lbs to 160lbs for the young fighter, and then up to 215lbs for the flabby older man. This isn't acting but, as De Niro has said, it made him feel different and perform differently. As to the fight scenes themselves, they were brilliantly shot from the point of view of those in the ring rather than the spectators. It was heightened, precisely choreographed realism, since even La Motta was less frenetic than this in the ring. But it provided the drama without which you would not be able to discern why the boxer was what he was outside the ring.

Schrader's original script was even darker and much more sexual than the finished film. At one point La Motta, who abstained from sex for several weeks before a big fight, douses an erection with a glass of cold water. Everyone liked the scene, but it would almost certainly have made *Raging Bull* into an X-rated film and it was never used. As it is, the film looks perfect, imbued with a European sensibility, as someone once said of Scorsese, but 'molto Hollywood'.

PICKPOCKET

Directed by Robert Bresson
With Martin Lasalle, Marika Green, Pierre Leymarie, Jean Pelegri
France, 1959, 75 minutes

Jean Pelegri, one of the non-professional actors in Bresson's *Pickpocket*, said of his director: 'He knows what he wants but he doesn't know why. Nobody could be less dogmatic or more obstinate than he. He relies entirely on his instinct.'

Most people think that Bresson, one of the few film-makers who never had to compromise for commercial purposes, was an intellectual who knows precisely why he wants what he wants. Which is partly why not everybody warms to his rigour and severity. But there's no doubt that he was a unique film-maker, and that *Pickpocket* is one of his masterworks.

It is, at base, about self-fulfilment and redemption through love – a common enough idea in films. But this 1959 epic has seldom been equalled as a philosophical treatise on the subject. The point is that the film is as much a visual argument as a spoken one.

His actors don't act, or even react, in any conventional sense, though Martin Lassalle's haunted persona is pretty magnetic throughout. They simply inhabit the story. And his settings are not so much naturalistic as adjuncts to what Bresson is trying to say. No one would argue, for instance, that Bresson's later *Lancelot du Lac*, the story of the lovers Lancelot and Guinevere, is an historically accurate view of the Middle Ages. But it is still a powerful commentary on the impossible quest for the grail and the ultimate failure of feudal society.

Michel (Lasalle) is a petty thief who, after being arrested and then released, starts discussing the rights and wrongs of crime with the police inspector. The only way he can find a place for himself in society is to engineer a head-on collision with it. It gives him a reason to live. In that way picking pockets becomes an exciting, almost sexual, adventure. It is a kind of pact with the Devil. But he has to leave France for London when the band of thieves he joins is arrested. And when he returns he is also caught. It is only when Jeanne (Marika Green), the girl who looked after his mother before she died and is now abandoned with a child, visits him in prison that he realises that his whole life could be changed by love. The humiliation of prison inspires him to a desperate act of faith.

The story is told in the form of Michel's diary, almost exclusively in mid and long shots with minimal camera movements and fade-outs as an alternative to editing. The eighteenth-century music of Lully is behind it. Only once does another way of working come into it when Bresson, who was fascinated by the methods used by pickpockets, describes the operations of a gang among the crowds at a railway station.

He also pays great attention to the sounds of the city, which resound in the small apartment in which Michel lives. The Longchamp races frame the story, and one notable sequence follows another, so that the parable grips even at its most internal.

Bresson is clearly not a film-maker for everybody, but he has pursued his own way remorselessly for the best part of 40 years, and he has a very faithful audience. His literary adaptations – from Giraudoux, Diderot, Bernados ad Dostoyevsky – are often merely points of departure. For him, 'the most important ideas in a film are the most hidden', so that the watcher has to look hard to find them. It is not an easy process, but it is a rewarding one since you feel he has a profound, and actually rather romantic, understanding of what he is talking about.

Added to that is his mastery of the medium – the way he has perfected a style that could be said to be completely unorthodox, easy to parody but almost impossible to copy.

His films have little or nothing to do with those of the French New Wave, but a lot to do with his Catholic background and the fact that he spent 18 months in a German prison camp during the Second World War.

Prison features not only in *Pickpocket* but in *Les Anges du Peche, Un Condamne à Mort* and *The Trial of Joan of Arc*. And most of his central characters seem imprisoned, if only in the soul, either through their misfortunes or because society has made it inevitable. If this seems a gloomy journey through which to travel, there are always points in his films where redemption and exaltation prevent glumness.

GREED

Produced and directed by Erich von Stroheim
With ZaSu Pitts, Gibson Gowland, Jean Hersholt
USA, 1926

There is nobody now alive who has seen anything like the complete version of von Stroheim's *Greed*. Yet many good judges still anoint the bleeding remains of the film as one of the greatest ever made. They are almost certainly right. But then Stroheim, better known to film-goers for his acting as Gloria Swanson's butler in Billy Wilder's *Sunset Boulevard* and the prison-camp commandant in Renoir's *Grand Illusion*, was one of the most extraordinary film-makers of all time.

Greed was to have been the culmination of his career – a virtually page-by-page adaptation of Frank Norris' tragic tale of McTeague, a former miner who, after succeeding as a dentist in San Francisco, loses his livelihood because of a rival's machinations, becomes a drunk and murders his wife. He kills his nemesis Marcus in a Death Valley shoot-out, but is bound to the corpse by handcuffs.

Von Stroheim's first cut ran to 47 reels, the one presented to the Goldwyn Company was 42, which he reduced on their request to 24, and then, helped by his friend Rex Ingram, to 18. The eventual release version, edited by June Mathis, Goldwyn's story editor who, Stroheim complained, hadn't read either the book or the original screenplay, was cut to a mere ten.

Years later, Henri Langlois, the great head of the Paris Cinématheque, showed Stroheim the mutilated version. He wept as he watched it and afterwards said: 'This was like an exhumation for me. In a tiny coffin I found a lot of dust, a terrible smell, a little backbone and a shoulder bone'. It was still, Langlois assured him, a masterpiece, even with its continuity gaps bridged by long titles. But what might it have been!

It isn't always true that the director's cut is invariably the best. But in Stroheim's case, dogged as he was throughout his Hollywood career by Irving Thalberg in particular – who once called him a footage fetishist – and commercial considerations that frequently cauterised his work, you could say that he remains a great film-maker despite the most appalling provocations.

Orson Welles, an admirer, described his art as Jewish baroque, and that tells some of the story (the von was apparently invented to hide his Jewish origins, as were his connections with the Austrian army and aristocracy). But *Greed* was more than that. It was a morality tale about the dehumanising influence of money, the stunning realism, vivid detail and complex characterisation of which made it unforgettable.

That he was an eccentric and extravagant egotist, and hard to deal with, is beyond question. But some of the rumours put about by his detractors were palpably exaggerations. It was said, for instance, that Stroheim once insisted upon the extras playing royal troops wearing the correct underwear. Perhaps he encouraged such legends. He certainly wanted authenticity above everything as he dissected his characters, their neuroses and their foibles.

André Bazin, the celebrated French critic, once wrote: 'In his films reality lays itself bare like a suspect confessing under the relentless examination of the commissioner of police. He has one simple rule for direction. Take a close look at the world, keep on doing so, and in the end it will lay bare for you all its cruelty and its ugliness.'

That is precisely what *Greed* does, with the aid of amazingly good performances from ZaSu Pitts and Gibson Gowland in particular. Sequence after sequence is stunning, like the one in which Pitts, as McTeague's wife, having won $5000 in a lottery, takes the gold coins from her mattress and caresses her naked body with them. That was typical Stroheim. Billy Wilder once told him he was ten years ahead of his time. 'No, twenty,' he replied. I'd say thirty.

DOUBLE INDEMNITY

Directed by Billy Wilder
With Fred MacMurray, Barbara Stanwyck, Edward G. Robinson
USA, 1944, 107 minutes

Someone once said that there was less in Billy Wilder than meets the eye. But actually there was more. What met the eye was usually pretty good. But it is often what meets the ear that's just as important. Where would *Double Indemnity*, *Sunset Boulevard* and *Some Like it Hot* be without their scripts, fashioned by him and marvellous writers like Charles Brackett, I.A.L. Diamond and, in the case of *Double Indemnity*, Raymond Chandler, the scion of the film noir genre?

What Wilder contributed was an ironic Viennese mordancy which is frequently copied today without the slightest idea of how to accomplish it properly, so that it all becomes parody. There is no parody even in *Some Like it Hot*, despite its highly satirical subject matter. But there would be if that film were remade now, as has occasionally been threatened.

Double Indemnity is a classic forties film of the sort which couldn't be made now without self-consciousness. Taken from James M. Cain's work, and actually made a good deal better by Chandler, who used to call Cain 'a Proust in overalls', it has the inimitable Fred MacMurray as an insurance agent seduced by Barbara Stanwyck's *femme fatale* in order to dispose of her husband for the 'double indemnity' insurance money.

The two work out a complicated scenario which, after the death of the husband, is gradually sussed by Edward G. Robinson's private investigator. On these melodramatic and not totally convincing bones, Wilder and Chandler construct a pitiless study of greed and perfidy – all the better because it is placed in such an ordinary, everyday American milieu.

It wasn't sexy, like *The Postman Always Rings Twice*, which Wilder always said was his model or testimonial. That wasn't possible in 1944 if you wanted to make a commercial movie that didn't worry the Paramount executives, and anyway Wilder invariably had as sharp an eye on what might get him into trouble as on his dialogue.

He's often been accused of trimming because of this. But the fact that you don't see much love-making in *Double Indemnity* is actually a strength, because it forces you to understand that it isn't sexual but financial lust that is the real motive behind the pair's clever, though not quite clever enough, planning fiasco.

The film is marvellously acted, particularly by MacMurray, who was so often cast in relatively anodyne romantic roles that his all-American wholesomeness could become cloying . Here that persona was brilliantly exploited to show us the weakness behind it. Wilder always depended upon his casts a lot, because sometimes the characterisation wasn't as sharp as the dialogue.

It was exceedingly lucky that George Raft refused the MacMurray role. 'Where's the lapel?' Wilder remembers him saying, 'You know, when the guy flips his lapel over and shows his badge'. Meaning, of course, that he had been the good guy all the time. 'No lapel, no George Raft.'

Another factor which makes *Double Indemnity* exceptional is its humour and lightness of touch, which prevents what is a decidedly dark tale, illustrated by Miklós Rozsa's superb score (based on César Franck's symphony) subsiding into melodrama.

The scene where the insurance man first meets his nemesis – he's trying to renew his motor insurance with her husband – has Stanwyck at the top of the stairs dressed only in a towel. Eyeing her with some interest, he says: 'I'd hate to think of you getting a scratched fender when you're not covered'. Stanwyck replies: 'I know what you mean. I've been sunbathing.' 'Hope there weren't any pigeons around,' he observes.

Later, the world-weary Marlowe-like voice-over proclaims, as he drives away from the encounter: 'It was a hot afternoon and I can still remember the smell of honeysuckle all along that street. How could I have known that murder can sometimes smell like that?'

Wilder once proclaimed *Double Indemnity* his best film. Asked why, he said: 'It had the fewest mistakes'. He was probably right, though supporters of *Some Like it Hot* may not agree.

SPIRIT OF THE BEEHIVE

Directed by Victor Erice
With Ana Torrent, Fernando Fernan Gomez
Spain, 1978, 98 minutes

I once showed a dozen or so non-American films to students at the Royal College of Art who seemed to know little about world as opposed to Hollywood cinema. To my surprise, despite the fact that the list included work by Buñuel, Satyajit Ray and Mizoguchi, the film they fell in love with was Victor Erice's *Spirit of the Beehive*. It is, however, without doubt one of the most beautiful movies it is possible to see, and certainly just about the best ever made in Spain.

Set in the Castillian countryside around 1940, at a time when Franco had won the Civil War but was still hunting down Republican sympathisers, and made in 1973, when it was still necessary for Spanish film-makers to cloak any political messages in allegory, it has an eight-year-old girl called Ana, superbly played by Ana Torrent, as its central character.

She watches James Whale's *Frankenstein* at the local cinema in a tiny village and can't understand why Frankenstein kills the little girl he meets and seems to cherish by the lakeside. Isabel, her elder sister, tells her that nobody actually dies in movies. But she adds that the monster is really a spirit who can take on human form and be summoned up by closing her eyes and calling out: 'I'm Ana'. She has, she says, seen him in a deserted farmhouse near the village.

Ana is determined, egged on by her sister playing games with her susceptibilities, to invoke the spirit. Going across the deserted fields to the outhouse, she discovers a Republican fugitive in hiding and brings him food. For her, he is Frankenstein, and even though he is later found shot by the Civil Guard, she is certain that spirits don't die, goes out in the middle of the night, and dreams she meets him like the little girl in Whale's film. Brought back home by her distraught parents and put to bed, she goes to her bedroom window and whispers: 'I'm Ana... I'm Ana'.

The film can be construed in many ways but is, above all, an almost perfect summation of childhood imaginings. It is also about the pall the dictator Franco's long shadow cast over Spain. Ana's father, played with understated power by Fernando Fernan Gomez, has evidently been traumatised by his experiences in the Civil War, and is now a shadowy figure writing a treatise on bee-keeping, while his wife pens letters to a would-be lover, exiled in France. They are a family 'locked up in themselves', unable to avoid the depression that has descended in the aftermath of a bloody war.

The film is thus cloaked in quiet and sadness, through which its two children move as if in a dreamworld of their own. It is brilliantly shot in muted colours by the great Spanish cinematographer Luis Cuadrado. The series of dissolves with which he denotes the passing of time outside the makeshift village cinema where the children see *Frankenstein* is a particularly stunning sequence. But there are many.

Few know that Cuadrado was fighting partial blindness at the time, which makes his work all the more remarkable. There is also a haunting score by Luis de Pablo which sums up everything while underlining nothing. It is virtually impossible to get the sight and sound of the film out of one's mind after watching it.

But, of course, it is chiefly Erice's – a perfectly controlled and imagined first feature so painstakingly made that Elias Querejeta, one of Spain's most enlightened producers, worried that it would never be completed. To date, Erice has only made two more features: *South*, which is actually only half of the intended story but remarkable all the same, and *The Quince Tree Sun*, one of the most astonishing films about the process of painting ever conceived. He is undoubtedly a minor master, and one uses the word minor more in relation to his output than his talent.

FREAKS

Directed by Tod Browning
With Wallace Ford, Leila Hyams
USA, 1932, 61 minutes

It's difficult to see Tod Browning's *Freaks*, even though it has the reputation of being one of the masterpieces of baroque cinema. The film has
been more written about than watched. Yet the tramps' last supper in
Buñuel's *Viridiana* was said to have been inspired by it, and Max Ophuls,
Fellini, Bergman and a host of horror merchants are among those who
have inserted clips from *Freaks* into their films.

One of the reasons it is not shown much these days, even in repertory,
is the feeling that it would be politically incorrect to do so. After all, not
so long ago Werner Herzog's *Even Dwarfs Started Small*, a parable about an
institution of dwarfs who revolt against their fully-sized governor, was
picketed at the National Film Theatre. And *Freaks* was banned in many
countries – for some 30 years in Britain – as too graphic a display of humans
with the severest of physical disabilities. Certainly if a contemporary
director tried the same thing now, he or she would be in some trouble.

Yet Browning, who had run away from school to join a circus where
the 'freaks' performed, was chiefly concerned not to make his strange
cast, culled from the circus, objects of horror or pity but to show them in
such a matter-of-fact manner, without close-ups or dramatic music, that
you could even watch Randian, the 'Hindu living torso' without arms and
legs, light his own cigar without assistance.

The problem is that, for all his entirely laudable insistence that these
people are totally normal in their human reactions, Browning had a
thoroughly freakish tale to tell. The film is based on 'Spurs', Clarence
Robbins's short story, and had been somewhat surprisingly commissioned
by Irving Thalberg, the youthful President of MGM, who had noted the
success of Browning's *Dracula* and James Whale's *Frankenstein* from the
competing Universal Studios.

The film had thus to mix horror, or at least grotesquerie, with
Browning's attempt at social comment, and there's no doubt that it is the
final sequences that cause the trouble. Essentially this is the story of
Cleopatra, a beautiful trapeze artist, on whom the midget Hans, although
already engaged to another of his own size, has an almighty crush. She is,
in fact, having an affair with Hercules, the no-good strongman, and
laughs at Hans behind his back.

But when Cleopatra realises that Hans will come into a small fortune,
she marries him, though her true feelings are even shown at the wedding

celebration. When Hans falls ill, he discovers that the medicine she is giving him is poison, and eventually she and Hercules are chased through the forest by the avenging freaks. He is killed and she is mutilated, becoming half-woman, half-chicken and squawking like a bird.

Generally this horrific moment ends the film, but there are at least two other finales, intimating that Hans goes back to his original fiancee, either with joy or with regret at what he has lost.

While it is perfectly clear that Browning wants us to regard the beautiful Cleo and the crooked Hercules as the villains of the piece – selfish, greedy and cruel – the chase scene, with the circus performers crawling and slithering through the woods to get at them, does create both horror and unease. Cleo and her strongman see them as monsters, and so, at this point, do we.

There are also some blatant pieces of sexual innuendo. For instance, Venus the seal trainer says to Phroso the clown: 'You're a pretty good kid', to which he replies suggestively: 'You're darn right I am. But you should have caught me before my operation!' And when someone kisses one half of the Siamese twins on the lips, the other sister appears to be enjoying it as much. Both have fiancees, and you can't help thinking about what might happen in the marital bed.

But despite one's doubts, Browning's film succeeds in being, as one critic has put it, 'moving, harsh, poetic and genuinely tender'. It was undoubtedly before its time, and to date no one has equalled it. Browning himself never did, but then he never had a chance, since *Freaks* was a commercial flop and Thalberg regretted he hadn't listened to those at MGM who had warned him against the project. Now, however, it looks very much like a damning antidote to the cult of physical perfection and a tribute to the circus 'freaks' who made up its cast.

BLANCHE

Directed by Walerian Borowczyk
With Michel Simon, Ligia Branice
France, 1971, 92 minutes

Walerian Borowczyk, if remembered at all nowadays, is recalled for the wrong reasons. He has been regarded in this country as a pseudo-cultured pornographer ever since *The Beast*, which ends with a prolonged sexual encounter in a forest between what looks like a large and well-hung ape and a woman, was shown at the National Film Theatre to a packed and pretentiously horrified audience. The film then came out commercially, minus most of the coupling, thanks to the Censor of the day.

It is true that Borowczyk, a Polish film-maker who has a small museum of historic erotic implements, about which he once made a wonderful little film, seems to have spent his last years in France, working in the soft-porn genre. But, if it is indeed true, as Nabokov says, that the letter 's' is the only difference between the cosmic and the comic, especially as far as sex is concerned, then some of us are right to regard him as a precious talent. Indeed, David Thomson, in his *Biographical Dictionary of Film*, calls him one of the major artists of the modern cinema.

Born in 1923, he started off as an animator of pinpoint delicacy and a kind of surreal edge that reminded one of Dada and Buñuel considerably more than Disney, and when he went into features there was the same eye for miniaturist detail, made to illustrate broader points. If his most 'infamous' films were *Immoral Tales* and *The Beast*, his most famous were *Goto, Isle of Love* and *Blanche*. Both of these are classics of their kind, starring Ligia Branice, then his wife and collaborator.

My favourite is *Blanche*, which also contains one of the last performances of the great Michel Simon – Renoir's *Boudu* and Vigo's *Jules*. And, when I showed it to a class of students who had never heard of Borowczyk or Simon, the film completely upended them. Admittedly it is weird enough to make them sit up and pay attention, and the musical score, just about the first to use period instruments, would almost certainly be immensely fashionable if put on record today.

It is set in thirteenth-century France, where Simon, who must have been well over eighty at the time, plays an almost senile baron who has married a simple but beautiful young wife (Branice) whom everyone, including the King, lusts after. There is a lecherous page and a handsome but rather vacant lover too, and the film is modelled as a kind of fairy-tale dance of death in which tragedy is probable even if a happy outcome isn't entirely out of the question.

Almost the whole film takes place in the Baron's castle, where the King comes to stay. And its winding stone staircases, gloomy corridors and rooms full of bizarre decor and even odder mechanical devices are as important as any characters in the film. Once again, every tiny detail is made to count double.

Blanche herself, who climbs naked out of her bath early in the film, thus gravely informing us exactly why sex may be part and parcel of the film, has a pet white dove in a cage which is almost her alter ego as she flutters round her admirers, half frightened and half fascinated. She is a creature made for trouble, and it isn't a total surprise when she is bricked into one of the castle's walls.

Borowczyk's art, which often looks like a carefully animated painting and has a pessimistic urge one might associate with Kafka, is invariably about sex, love and death – the orgasmic ape in *The Beast* eventually dies of pleasure. But his eye is so sharp and his ironic sense of humour so audacious that even the worst of his films, like *Emmanuelle 5*, are worth something. The best inhabit a world you are unlikely to forget.

BEYOND A REASONABLE DOUBT

Directed by Fritz Lang
With Dana Andrews, Joan Fontaine
USA, 1956, 80 minutes

I once went to a party in Hollywood for François Truffaut, who was one of the few French directors of whom Hollywood at that time had heard. There were a lot of high rollers there congratulating each other on their careers, but I was more curious about an old man with an eye-patch sitting alone in a corner.

When I asked who he was, someone said off-handedly: 'Oh, that's some old German director'. In fact, it was Fritz Lang who, apart from his German classics, had made a number of the very best American films of the forties and fifties. He had been invited largely because of Truffaut's long-held admiration for him, particularly of his American movies.

He seemed surprised that I knew most of his films, and asked me which I liked best. I replied *M* as the German example and *Beyond a Reasonable Doubt* as the American. But it could have been half a dozen other films.

Lang moved from an extraordinary mastery of European expressionism, allowing him to illustrate the state of a continent that gave rise to fascism, to an implicit critique of the 'freedom' of American capitalism. Perhaps he was a pessimist for whom life itself appeared to be some kind of trap. But he was indisputably a great director.

Beyond a Reasonable Doubt, in which the now underrated Dana Andrews gives one of his most effective performances, illustrates the second half of the equation perfectly. It is a film of great economy and precision (it lasts only 80 minutes), it has the terrifying inevitability of Greek tragedy and a pervading sense that man is his own worst enemy.

Andrews plays a reporter who agrees to incriminate himself in a murder case because his editor (Sidney Blackmer) is pursuing a campaign against capital punishment. They plant the lighter given to the reporter by his fiancee (Joan Fontaine) and the reporter then poses for the photographs that will prove his innocence.

Almost immediately Lang's long shot of the scene seems to suggest that things may go badly wrong. They do. He starts to seduce a stripper who was the murdered girl's friend, infuriating his own woman but confident that she'll understand when all is explained. But when the only man who can exonerate him is killed in a car accident, she fights to establish his innocence – only to find that he is, in fact, guilty.

This slightly tuppence-coloured story is so tautly directed and so skilful in its manipulation of our sympathies that, several times during the film, one changes sides, for and against the man who so tempted fate and the woman whose righteousness may be impeccable but is also more than a bit irritating.

The reason the film deserves its accolades as much as *The Big Heat*, *You Only Live Once* and *Rancho Notorious* is at least in part the fact that Lang takes a simple format and makes it beautifully complicated. The form is one thing, the content another in most movies. In this it is utterly indivisible.

The career of Lang is ample evidence that it is not true that most European directors who went to America were destroyed by the system, though many were undoubtedly hampered by it. Europe itself did its share of destruction.

Born in Vienna, Lang's *Testament of Dr Mabuse*, another great film, was banned by the Nazis, after which he was summoned to the office of Joseph Goebbels, the propaganda minister, and apologetically asked to supervise Nazi film production.

Fearing his Jewish background would be discovered – one of the traps so often set for characters in his films – he fled Germany. But it's only fair to add that he also fled Hollywood in 1956, citing continual disputes with producers as his reason.

Nevertheless, he made great films in two continents – in three actually, if you subscribe to the view that *The Tiger of Eschnapur*, made in India, is a successful mixture of his German and American styles. That's a pretty extraordinary record.

CUBA SI!

Directed and photographed by Chris Marker
France, 1961, 90 minutes

Documentarists tend to be an eccentric breed. They need to be, since none of the main film festivals allow their films into competition (surely an incomprehensible decision), and to get a documentary into a cinema these days, or even onto television unless it is controlled by the station, is a fraught process. But there is no more highly personal yet elusive film-maker than Chris Marker. His importance lies not in how many audiences have been affected by his films but how many of his fellow film-makers regard him as something of a genius.

It would be possible to choose half a dozen of his films as classics, and I only select the 1961 *Cuba Si!* because its importance at the time was so obvious. It remains just about the best and most intimate film on the making of a revolution that exists. And one writes 'highly personal' in describing Marker with some justice as far as *Cuba Si!* is concerned, since he has the cheek to insert shots from an old Robin Hood movie during his interview with Fidel Castro.

Marker's preface to the script is illuminating. 'Shot rapidly in January, 1961, during the first alert period (you know, at the time when the majority of French papers were hooting over Fidel's paranoia in imagining himself threatened with invasion) it aims at communicating, if not the experience, at least the vibrations, the rhythm of a revolution that will one day perhaps be held to be the decisive moment of a whole era of contemporary history.

'It also aims at countering the monstrous wave of misinformation in the major part of the press. It is interesting that it was the same Minister who tolerated in the press and sanctioned on the radio the most outrageous untruths at the moment of the invasion of April, 1961, who had the nerve to ban *Cuba Si!* in the name of historical truth...'

As you can see, Marker has always been a slightly ironic polemicist and was for many years a Marxist, or at least a left-leaning radical. He was born of an aristocratic family – his real name is Bouche-Villeneuve – in Mongolia in 1921, but he tends to keep his early life a secret. What isn't a secret is his extreme modesty and dislike of fake celebrity, which means few festivals see him in attendance and even fewer interviewers get to question him.

He sees himself merely as a concerned and inquisitive traveller, reporting back to the world on what he has found. He is, however, much more than that. His intelligence and perceptiveness, and his great knowledge of the cinema, history and culture render him no ordinary observer with access to a camera.

Marker has been to Peking, Russia, Tokyo and Israel as well as Cuba but, though a leftist member of the French Resistance during the Second World War, his views on Castro's tight little island are by no means orthodox. It is the capacity of ordinary Cubans to live like kings despite every deprivation that strikes him forcibly. Their vitality, expressed in their music (as evidenced by Wim Wenders's *Buena Vista Social Club*), gives him as much hope as anything in Castro's political credo.

Perhaps what makes Marker so valuable as a recorder of slices of our time is the fact that he is also a writer and poet who in another time might have been a keeper of journals like Johnson or Goethe. It was not for nothing that someone once called him 'our unknown cosmonaut'. *Cuba Si!*, like so many of his films – *Lettre de Siberie*, *Le Joli Mai*, *La Jetée* and *Sans Soleil*, for instance – seems to discover what everyone else has missed. That, of course, is what the best kind of film-maker is supposed to do.

LA FEMME INFIDELE

Directed by Claude Chabrol
With Stephane Audran, Michel Bouquet, Maurice Ronet
France, 1970, 98 minutes

Nowadays, you never know what you are going to get from Claude Chabrol. There was, however, a short spell in the late sixties and early seventies when you knew exactly. From the 1968 *Les Biches* to the 1971 *Juste Avant la Nuit,* he made half a dozen psychological thrillers that have never been equalled, at least by a European director.

Even Hitchcock, whose name has often been mentioned as Chabrol's inspiration, would be hard pressed to beat the cool certainty of Chabrol's technique, and the emotional heat he generated while examining the underbelly of the always well-fed French bourgeoisie.

Most of these films starred the fine-boned and striking Stephane Audran, then his wife, and all of them were shot by the great Jean Rabier – forming a trio who perfectly complemented each other. And one way to describe this posse of classics would be to say that they were among the most civilised depictions of highly uncivilised behaviour ever to reach the screen.

My favourite, not necessarily the best, is one of the simplest – *La Femme Infidèle*, in which Chabrol displays an irrestistible logic and an ironic humour that never gets in the way of the horrific implications of the story.

Michel Bouquet is the husband who suspects his wife of having a lover, gradually discovers that he is right, and not entirely on purpose kills the man (Maurice Ronet). He then has to get rid of the body without telling his wife (Audran). But she discovers, and eventually so do the police.

Instead of giving him away, however, the *femme infidèle*, realising how much he loves her, keeps mum. They are, after all, both culpable. Finally, however, the evidence against him is too great and he has to give himself up.

He leaves her with the words: 'I love you madly', and we believe she loves him too. This is a very emotional film, but the way Chabrol depicts that emotion is cumulative rather than baldly stated. The control is absolute throughout, and it makes the finale all the more moving.

One of the best sequences, which manages to be very funny as well as heart-stopping, is when the husband, having used a private detective, decides to introduce himself to the lover. He is polite and matter-of-fact at first.

But as the unsuspecting lover, lulled by the husband's attitude, expounds on the extraordinary nature of the woman with whom he is infatuated, nerve-ends snap and the murder results. We see that the husband never really knew his wife, and that's where his anger comes from, rather than the act of infidelity itself.

Another amazing section of the film concerns this urbane man's efforts to cover up all traces of his crime, cleaning the flat, dragging the body to his car in a weighted sack and finally heaving it into a nearby lake. This has been done so often before in films, but seldom with a greater sense of what such an awful process must be like.

But, all the way through, what could have been just another thriller becomes much more than that. It is also a passionate love story, with its share of intense irony and a pervading sense of the quirkiness of fate.

Perhaps the most famous of these six films made between 1968 and 1971 is *Le Boucher* (*The Butcher*), in which a psychotic village butcher is driven to murder by his unrequited passion for the local schoolteacher (Audran again). This could be an even better film than *La Femme Infidèle*. But then Chabrol seemed to be at the height of his very considerable powers during this fruitful period.

Of course Hitchcock, whom he greatly admired, was a considerable influence on his best work, particularly as Chabrol examines the nature of guilt and more often than not decides that the victim is as culpable as the so-called criminal.

But Chabrol was a different kind of stylist, equally cynical but basically more of a humorist and thus more humane. I once had lunch with him in Paris, an amusing affair at which murder was nearly committed when the time came to pay the bill. 'Oh and by the way,' he said on parting from a studious British critic who always praised his work in very intellectual terms, 'Give my regards to __. He invents my films so beautifully'.

THE LIFE AND DEATH OF COLONEL BLIMP

Directed by Michael Powell
With Roger Livesey, Deborah Kerr, Anton Walbrook
UK, 1943, 163 minutes

I was once asked at the Cannes Festival to provide, at short notice when Dirk Bogarde cried off, a tribute to Michael Powell in front of an international assemblage much more distinguished than myself. Powell himself was there, and I took my courage into my hands and said that, among those present were a good many from the British film industry who had once done their best to decry the work of one of Britain's most justly celebrated film-makers.

It was, of course, after the making of 1960's *Peeping Tom*, Powell's most controversial film, that he was attacked, not only by the industry but by most of the British critics. Even before that, however, his extraordinary capacity to make utterly British films with some of the imagination and sensibility of Buñuel made him more suspect than contemporaries like Hitchcock, David Lean and Carol Reed.

His achievement, mostly in concert with Emeric Pressburger, writer and producer, was immense, and his reputation is now finally secure, thanks in part to the consistent advocacy of Americans like Martin Scorsese, who recognised a genius when they saw one. It would be perfectly in order to choose any of five or six films to present among one's personal best.

I choose *The Life and Death of Colonel Blimp* not because it is perfect but because it raised so many awkward questions at the time of its making during World War II that Winston Churchill tried to have it banned. It typifies Powell's almost always totally unorthodox approach to the conventions of British film-making. It was the film that one American critic has called 'the British *Citizen Kane*', but in truth it is more of a tribute to the paradoxical nature of the British character, generally masked by the stiff-upper-lipped films of the time.

The film uses extensive flashbacks to trace the lives of a young British officer and his German counterpart from the time when they fought a duel in the Berlin of 1902 to the middle of the Second World War, when Roger Livesey's Major General Clive Wynne-Candy VC has become a blimpish old buffer (the character is based upon the cartoonist Low's Colonel Blimp) and Anton Walbrook's gallant German officer arrives as a refugee from the Nazis. They are now fast friends, even though Wynne-Candy has lost his one true love (Deborah Kerr) to the German. Kerr also plays the other two women in his life, none of them ultimately obtainable – the part of the film which gives it its romantic, elegiac if pessimistic edge.

Churchill's reaction was furious. He is said to have stormed into Walbrook's dressing room when he was appearing in a West End play and demanded: 'What's this film supposed to mean? I suppose you regard it as good propaganda for Britain?' But the film, while mourning the death of the Colonel Blimps of Britain, because of their old-fashioned virtues of decency and generosity, admits its necessity. We should, it suggests, finally leave the past but never forget its better aspects.

This was interpreted as 'black-hearted bitterness against Britain' in some quarters, but, when the film was revived during the British Film Year of 1985 it received almost unanimous acclaim, often mistakenly, with several critics praising it for recognising a time when there was pride in being British. The fact is that it is the emotional tensions in Powell's work that renders it exceptional.

All this would be as nothing had he not been, admittedly much aided by Pressburger, a film-maker of great technical and imaginative ability who could shape his stories with such flair that you couldn't recognise a cliche even if it stared you in the face.

Admittedly Colonel Blimp is too long, but Powell's almost expressionistic use of colour (aided by cinematographer Jack Cardiff), his feeling that fantasy often holds more truth than reality, and his generosity of spirit towards both his central characters, triumphs over the film's flaws. So too does the magnificent performance of Livesey as Blimp, a part once scheduled for Olivier, who would surely have rendered it more of a parody. It is a great British film, and there haven't been too many of those.

THE RISE TO POWER OF LOUIS XIV

Directed by Roberto Rossellini
With Jean-Marie Patte, Raymond Jourdan, Silvagni, Katharina Renn
Italy/France, 1966, 90 minutes

No director I have had the good fortune to meet impressed me more than Roberto Rossellini. He talked with such eloquence and passion about film that you could readily believe there was no greater nor more diverse art. For him, its roots sprung from a documentary tradition he extended as widely as possible, and my choice of his films is one which perfectly illustrates what you can do in this genre – his 1966 *The Rise to Power of Louis XIV*.

The most influential of the Italian neo-realists, whose work came to be so admired in the post-war period, and which even today is regarded with almost religious fervour in what we used to call the Third World, he was also the director who most thoroughly transcended that label.

It wasn't *Rome, Open City* or *Paisa* that made Godard, for instance, acknowledge his influence, great as both these films were. The fact is that any literate film-maker, even those whose work is restricted to television, like part of Rossellini's, would be hard put to deny it. It isn't much of an exaggeration to say that after him film could never be quite the same again.

He could make bad films, or least films which were at first badly misunderstood, like the extraordinary *Stromboli* and *Voyage to Italy*, two of five films made with his lover Ingrid Bergman – an affair which shocked the world and almost ruined him. But his greatness lay in his ability to make those who watched his films into active participants. There was no way you can be simply entertained by Rossellini. You had to become involved.

Lionel Trilling called him a highly politicised intellectual, but he was also a philosopher of cinema, and certainly his series of didactic reconstructions of history, of which *The Rise to Power of Louis XIV* is the most perfectly achieved, emphasised that.

The film opens with the sickness and death of the powerful and virtually regal Cardinal Mazarin, and concentrates on Louis's successful seizure and retention of power. Almost everything depicted in it, and much of the dialogue, comes directly from documents of the period. But

it is also informed by a particularly Rossellinian sensibility, with which he contrasts the ambitious machinations of this world with the inevitability of decay and death.

The demise of Mazarin is brilliantly handled – the doctors sniffing the old man's sweat and faeces before they bleed him through the foot; Mazarin refusing to see the young King before applying rouge to his ashen cheeks, like one consummate actor facing another. The triumph of appearance over reality is everywhere apparent since, as Machiavelli stated, 'ordinary people are always deceived by appearances'.

Later, with Louis triumphant at the end of the film, we see the King alone in his chambers, now Le Roi Soleil, having taken off his royal clothes and the wig which makes him look taller, reading aloud from La Rochefoucauld: 'Neither the sun nor death can be looked firmly in the face'.

Both long sequences illustrate that this is not just a history lesson or a piece of semi-Brechtian polemic, but a dramatic and acutely personal reflection on how the successful acquisition of power is always transient. But the method of gaining that temporary control is brilliantly laid out before us, with impeccable visual and verbal logic.

Rossellini manages this by utilising costumes, decor, architecture, mise-en-scene and some amazing colour photography in order to illustrate how Louis created a hierarchy that would render his nobles helplessly enmeshed in climbing up and down a slippery pole, often bankrupted in the process.

The whole makes one deeply regret that Rossellini died before he could make his projected film about Marx, since such a grasp of social and cultural history and such a feeling for how individuals make it might have enlightened us far better than any Russian hagiography or grudging Western homage.

He did, however, make similar projects about Socrates, Garibaldi, Pascal, Descartes, St Francis and St Augustine. *Louis XIV*, however, was the most extraordinary. It remains the film which should be studied not only by anyone interested in the cinema but by anyone attempting the fictionalised documentaries that have been so devalued on television recently. Rossellini never cheated. He attempted simply to explain.

LE SAMOURAI

Directed by Jean-Pierre Melville
With Alain Delon, François Perier, Nathalie Delon
France, 1967, 95 minutes

In France, there are few more admired directors than Jean-Pierre Melville, an extraordinary talent who was thought by many to be the real ancestor of the French New Wave, but was affected as much by the American cinema as his own. He changed his name from Grumbach after reading *Moby Dick*, and used to wear a Stetson and dark glasses, as if to prove his allegiance to American style. But though Hollywood films, especially of the pre-war variety, were his model, his own work remained unmistakably French. In fact, many thought he was as much influenced by Bresson as by films such as Huston's *Asphalt Jungle*. He would usually reply that, on the contrary, Bresson was influenced by him.

Certainly, he made a whole series of films that were unlike anyone else's, and *Le Samourai*, one of the best of them, could easily be regarded as one of the greatest psychological thrillers, addressing questions of honour, loyalty and betrayal. It gave Alain Delon the best part he ever had.

Filmed on the wide screen, and in wonderfully muted colour to add atmosphere – the great Henri Decae was Melville's cinematographer – it has Delon as a ruthless and efficient hired killer living alone in a dingy apartment with a bullfinch as his sole companion. The girl who loves him (Nathalie Delon, then Alain's wife) lives in more luxury elsewhere at another man's expense, and is prepared to give him a perfect alibi after his next contract. He executes it with chilling skill in a nightclub and then successfully avoids both a hood sent to kill him and a posse of police on his trail.

He is, however, doomed from the first, or, as Melville puts it, 'laid out in death'. He is tempted by a girl he saw in a corridor of the nightclub and should have killed as a witness, thus destroying the first rule of the samurai, which is not to get emotionally involved. It's a bad mistake, and honour demands that she has to be his next contract. But, almost masochistically, he deliberately uses an empty gun and is shot down by the police. He has virtually committed *hara-kiri*.

It is difficult to see how this story could be better accomplished. It has all the best virtues of the American film noir but also a European sensibility which might have seemed either melodramatic or pretentious in a Hollywood film. Paris becomes a city of shadows, like Cocteau's *zone de la mort* and, in the very first scene, where Delon lies stretched out on his bed in the half-light, a sense of acute foreboding is created. This is rigorously maintained throughout with very little dialogue to disturb it.

Added to that, Melville shows us his lone killer's precise and methodical methods with great cinematic flair and, in particular, makes the police manhunt through the Metro from which he eventually escapes into as good an action sequence as any in those contemporary films which specialise in them. *Le Samourai* is as efficient a piece of cinema as it is darkly romantic. And Delon's deliberately impassive performance has its measure.

When Melville offered the part to Delon and started reading him the screenplay, the actor listened for some time before saying: 'You've been reading the script for seven and a half minutes now and there hasn't been a word of dialogue. That's good enough for me. I'll do it.' *Le Samourai* opens with a purported line from the *Book of Bushido* – 'There is no greater solitude than that of the Samurai, unless perhaps it be that of the tiger in the jungle'. Delon expresses that perfectly.

Later, after the film was shown in Japan, Melville admitted that he wrote the quotation himself. It wasn't for nothing that Godard gave him a bit part in *Breathless*. He and other New Wavers acknowledged his mastery freely, while understanding that he was an individualist who would never subscribe to any cinematic or political movement.

SONS OF THE DESERT

Directed by William A. Seiter
With Stan Laurel, Oliver Hardy, Charley Chase, Mae Busch
USA, 1933, 68 minutes

Not everybody finds Laurel and Hardy funny. Those who do, however, adore them. I am one of that number – the greater fan because, as a small boy, I actually met them in their London dressing room during their post-war theatrical tour of Britain. They generously entertained me with tea, buns and jokes for nearly an hour and I've never forgotten it.

At that time, they had rather gone out of fashion – the hall was only half full, which was perhaps why they were grateful for a young fan. But now they have become recognised again as two of the greatest cinema clowns, whose 'duet of incompetence' inspired dozens of two-reelers and a posse of admittedly more uneven features whose most cherishable moments will never be forgotten.

The best of them was *Sons of the Desert*, though some would nominate *Way Out West* instead. As for the shorts, look at the Academy Award-winning *The Music Box* and you'll see true comic genius.

As a generalisation, it could be said that the British-born Stan Laurel was the ideas man who thought up gags, planned stories and wanted a hand in direction, while Oliver Hardy was the fall-guy who, the director Leo McCarey once said, 'had difficulty finding his way to the studio', generally from the golf course. Laurel, in fact, was always paid more than Hardy.

The situation, however, was often reversed on screen. Laurel in squeaky, complaining tears was wonderful, but nobody could do a double-take or manage a pearler like Ollie. It wasn't just the impeccable timing. It was the sense of upended dignity he invariably conveyed. He was the daintiest fat man who ever existed, capable with one long look of portraying a world of appalling injustice.

Sons of The Desert provides some fodder for the idea that they had a misogynist's view of women. In it, both their wives are aggressive and unsympathetic. Mae Bush's Mrs Hardy is not averse to throwing kitchen-ware at her husband, while Mrs Laurel (Dorothy Christie) feels she has to act like a duck-hunting male to compensate for the feebleness of her husband. The two men spend half of the film avoiding the consequences of their actions as far as the two women are concerned.

Their main subterfuge is to persuade their wives that Ollie has to go on a vacation to Honolulu for health reasons – 'I think he's suffering from a nervous shakedown,' says Stan. In fact, they are off to the Chicago annual meeting of the Sons of the Desert, an organisation parodying both the Masons and a Shriner's convention.

The comedy is based on character rather than many of the comic routines which made the pair famous in the silent days, and the dialogue isn't so much witty as totally dependent on their capacity to portray rather glorious fools. 'All work and no play makes Jack a dull boy,' says Ollie as if he thought up the phrase himself in attempting to persuade his wife to let him go. But the whole thing is ruined when Stan says: 'Jack who?' It's not the words but the attendant pantomime that's important.

The whole tightly controlled film shows the pair at their best, fighting to maintain their dignity in a world which is actually almost as absurd as they are. Few other comedy duos have created and maintained characters of such loveable dimensions, even if a lot of the films they made were no more than pedestrian vehicles for their best qualities. They seemed in their movies virtually married to one another – a fact which has led some critics to suggest homosexual implications. Sex, however, was never on their agenda like it was on that of the Marx Brothers or Crosby and Hope. Instead, there was a long-suffering affection between the two, a kind of wounded liaison against the world which was not only exceedingly funny but somehow moving too.

THE STORY OF THE LATE CHRYSANTHEMUMS

Directed by Kenji Mizoguchi
With Shotaro Hanayagi, Kakuko Mori
Japan, 1939, 142 minutes

When the National Film Theatre last mounted a retrospective of the work of Kenji Mizoguchi, the first for many years, it was so well attended that several of the Japanese director's most notable films were successfully released on the art circuit. The retrospective even beat the record set by the Howard Hawks season at the same London venue. However much of a surprise that was, the fact is that Mizoguchi can sit confidently beside Hawks as one of the greatest film-makers of all time.

Yet, unlike Hawks, only about a third of his work survives, since the Japanese were for many years careless about their extraordinary cinematic legacy – remember that Kurosawa was so neglected that he tried to commit suicide. Mizoguchi himself said he made 'only about 75 films or so – not really very many'. And in defence of the Japanese, it is certain that some of them were destroyed during the wartime fire raids on Tokyo.

It is extremely difficult to select just one of the remaining masterworks to represent him. *Ugetsu Monogatari* is the film in many critics' ten best lists, *The Life of O-Haru* is the epic generally thought to express best his innate sympathy for women. My favourite, however, is *Zangiku Monogatari* – *The Story of the Late Chrysanthemums*, possibly because it was the first Mizoguchi I saw and it has stuck in my mind ever since.

In essentials, this is the sad story of a woman from a lower class than her actor lover who sustains his faltering career and then sacrifices herself to ensure his success. Donald Ritchie, the critic who was among the first to tell the West about Mizoguchi, says that, just as Ford put John Wayne and Ward Bond in place of himself in his films, so the Japanese director indentified with his chosen actresses. He got superb performances from them, but at a price, since he was a perfectionist who sometimes caused them infinite pain. He didn't make films for women but about them.

Nicknamed 'the Demon', it was often said that he only made films to have enough money to entertain geishas, and he was certainly fascinated all his life by demi-mondaines, inhabitants of what was called the floating world. One critic has said that he would have been the perfect director to make a movie of Puccini's *Madame Butterfly*. Others have suggested that there was something suspect about his compassion for the often tragic fate of such women. Even so, he hardly gloats over the fate of the woman in *Late Chrysanthemums*. Instead, he remorselessly shows the selfishness of her actor lover and the innate snobbism of the Kabuki world.

He falls for her, a wet nurse in his wealthy household, perhaps because she is the only one to tell him his acting is terrible. Together they enter the wilderness of third-rate acting companies and, thanks to her, his talent develops and engagements in Tokyo beckon. The sequence during which the woman, now dying, watches the actor's triumph as he passes her by on a carnival riverboat, is one of the most moving in all cinema, heightened as we see first the actor's bows to the applauding crowds and then his face suddenly covered with guilt.

But social criticism is only part of his films. If he was the poet of women, he was also the poet of houses and rooms, landscapes and urban vistas. His period detail and his sumptuous camera style lent his stories a kind of fantastic naturalism, added to by an almost musical editing style. He was capable of virtually everything from waspish comedy to tenderness, the most intimate of scenes to epic sequences of battle. A director for all seasons, in fact, whom Kurosawa, much better known in the West, freely acknowledged was his master.

I cannot tell you how important Mizoguchi was to my film-going experience. He made me realise what the art of the cinema could achieve. And his films will live with vibrant life for as long as anyone watches other than Hollywood movies.

THE KING OF MARVIN GARDENS

Directed by Bob Rafelson
With Jack Nicholson, Bruce Dern, Ellen Burstyn
USA, 1972, 104 minutes

It took some time to decide whether to put Bob Rafelson's *Five Easy Pieces* or his later *The King of Marvin Gardens* into this list. Both films, made in the early seventies, starred Jack Nicholson and expressed through him the particularly American angst of the period. Begging Marlon Brando and Elia Kazan's pardon, you could call it the 'I don't want to be a contender' syndrome.

In *Five Easy Pieces*, Nicholson plays a man whose middle name is Eroica, after Beethoven, and who once studied to be a concert pianist, but rejects his middle-class aspirations in favour of a messy life as an oilfield rigger. In *The King of Marvin Gardens* he is an introspective all-night talk jock whose brief hope of getting away from it all resides in his brother's moonshine plan to win a lucrative gambling concession in Hawaii.

Both films are funny, poetic and touchingly observant of the kind of American society you don't often see on film. But they are deeply melancholy at the same time, as if there's no rational reason for their characters to behave as they do, only cracked emotional ones. It's not so much the American dream gone sour as a total rejection of that fairytale concept.

Rafelson had a great success with *Five Easy Pieces*, which pitched Nicholson into stardom every bit as much as *Easy Rider*. But the more tragic and acutely personal *Marvin Gardens* is perhaps ultimately the more reverberating film, crashing into tragedy with a ludicrous murder at its end. In any case, Rafelson, hard as he continued to try, in particular with *Stay Hungry* and *The Postman Always Rings Twice*, never managed the same amazing grace again.

What made *Marvin Gardens* so good was the dove-tailed playing of Nicholson as the talk radio man and Bruce Dern as his conman brother – hopeless cases who can't manage their lives or the equally well drawn women who come into contact with them. Dern lives with Ellen Burstyn's ageing blonde and her pretty step-daughter (Julia Anne Robinson), and the film achieves a sexual contest between them that ends in the murder. But not before an extraordinary scene where the older woman throws all her clothes and make-up, including her prized mink eyelashes, onto a bonfire on the beach.

Rafelson's portrait of a wintry Atlantic City is of a down-at-heel holiday and gambling resort which seems to point up the characters' disillusionment. Only Louis Malle, in *Atlantic City*, orchestrated a tale in such accurately crestfallen waters.

Rafelson, it has been said, is 'a raconteur of vivid, touching events, himself looking on from the dark'. And in both films what we see are people we can't dislike, and who seem very real, struggling to make sense of lives which have ceased to be capable of the kind of redemption they clumsily seek. But it isn't depressing seeing this up on the screen. There's too much edgy plotting and seemingly improvised and truthful dialogue for that.

It's possible that after an extraordinary beginning, which included the inventive Monkees film *The Head* – he had created the group himself for a TV show – Rafelson's kind of highly personal cinema became more and more difficult to make. He was, for instance, thrown off the set of *Brubaker* for chucking a chair at an interfering Fox executive. More likely, however, times moved on without him. It happens to the best of directors as well as the worst. Few American film-makers, however, can count among their work two such resonant films as these.

TOKYO STORY

Directed by Yasujiro Ozu
With Chishu Ryo, Cheiko Higashiyama
Japan, 1953, 139 minutes

For those brought up on the energetic and sustaining diet of the American cinema, it may not be easy to appreciate the quietist art of the great Japanese director Yasujiro Ozu. He has been called the poet of family life, capable of taking the seemingly trivial and making great drama of it. Nothing was too small to be significant.

He steadfastly peered into the hearts and minds of his characters until we feel we know them intimately. And the loyalty of those who love his work is as absolute as his own conviction. The number of film-makers who have made pilgrimages to his grave (on which there is simply the Japanese word for 'nothing') runs into dozens.

Ozu started making films in 1927, and was one of the last to forsake the silent cinema. Much of this early work is lost or destroyed. But we know from examples that he wasn't always as calmly contemplative as he was in his late work, which reached the West only in the sixties. He could make boisterous comedies and earthy chronicles of family life, containing outrageous sight gags. In the last stretch of his life, however, he had refined his art so much that it hardly seemed like art at all. But this simplicity hid the kind of patient sophistication that only a great artist can distil.

His most famous film, and certainly one of his masterpieces, was *Tokyo Story*. In it an elderly couple are taken to visit their grown-up children in Tokyo. Too busy to entertain them, the children pack them off to a noisy resort. Returning to Tokyo, the old woman visits the widow of another son, who treats her better, while the old man gets drunk with some old companions. They seem to realise they are a burden, and simply try to smooth things over as best they can.

By now the children have, albeit guiltily, given up on them, and even when their mother is taken ill and dies on the way home, they rush back to Tokyo after attending the funeral. A simple proverb expresses their failure – 'Be kind to your parents while they are alive. Filial piety cannot reach beyond the grave.' The last sequence is of the old man alone in his seaside home, followed by an outside shot of the rooftops of the town and a boat passing by on the water. Life goes on.

The film condemns no one, and its sense of inevitability carries with it only a certain resigned sadness. 'Isn't life disappointing,' someone says at one point. Yet its simple observations are so acute that you feel that no other film will ever be able to express its subject matter much better.

Ozu shoots his story with as little movement of the camera as possible. We view scenes almost always looking up from the floor, lower than the eye level of a seated character. For this reason, the director usually insisted on ceilings to his sets. As for the actors, he insisted that no one was to dominate a scene and that control was everything. The balance of every scene had to be perfect.

Chishu Ryo, who often played the father in Ozu's films about family life, once had to complete two dozen takes devoted to how a teacup was raised to his lips and put down. In the end there was not much editing to be done.

Tokyo Story was followed by eight other films, all of them as masterful, and a group named after the seasons, like *Early Spring, Late Autumn, The End of Summer* and *An Autumn Afternoon*. Each was about the problems of ordinary family life – the last-named a classic about a gentle widower who arranges the marriage of the daughter who looks after him, and is left with the realisation that he is alone and growing old.

While the essentially conservative nature of these films made the younger, more polemical Japanese directors, like Imamura and Oshima, impatient, their universality has come to be recognised. If Ozu was the most Japanese of film-makers, his appeal is easily able to cross most cultural barriers.

SHOAH

Directed by Claude Lanzmann
France, 1986, 563 minutes

The title of this more than nine-hour-long documentary is a Hebrew word for chaos or annihilation. In other words, the Holocaust. Yet there are no old newsreels, few interviews with survivors, and there is no coverage of war-crimes trials. Claude Lanzmann, the director, spent six years simply looking for eye-witnesses. Most of those witnesses are veteran Germans and Poles who either worked in the camps or observed from near at hand what went on in them.

The faces of those he interviewed are interspersed with sequences of the places where the deaths took place, not as they were but as they are now. Grass and flowers grow on the mass graves, the tracks on which the inmates were transported are still used by trains, and the concentration camps themselves look like harmless, disused factories. The horror is not what we see now but what we are told about the past.

Lanzmann poses as a patient, often kindly but insistent interrogator. He doesn't ask large questions but small ones. He simply tries to winkle out the details. No philosophy, and no moral strictures. It's simply what happened that counts – the how rather than the why. It is not always fair, since his methods are sometimes underhand, using concealed cameras or assuring people that their conversations with him are private. Generally, however, we see what they see – the cameras and the tall, lanky, chain-smoking man who asks the questions.

Nothing is formally arranged in the editing. *Shoah* is not a chronological or factual record of the Holocaust. We have survivors, those who killed and bystanders in a kind of mosaic which begins slowly to make sense of something utterly without sense. Ordinary people enmeshed in extraordinary times? Perhaps. But we get no clue from Lanzmann.

At one point he interviews a railway engineer who drove the trains to Treblinka and asks if he could hear what went on in the carriages behind his locomotive. Obviously, he could – 'The screams from the cars closest to the locomotives could be heard very well'.

'Can one get used to that?' asks Lanzmann. 'No,' says the engineer, recalling that the Germans gave him and other workers vodka to drink so that they could do the job.

There are many who never seemed to have witnessed or even comprehended the whole picture because they worked on only a small part of it, like scheduling the trains or organising work parties. There are more who must have guessed what was going on near their homes or farms but simply kept quiet. But there are some so closely involved that you can scarcely believe what you are hearing.

There is Filip Muller, the Czech Jew whose duty it was to stand at the crematorium doors at Auschwitz as the victims walked in. One day he saw a group of his own countrymen singing first the 'Hatikvah' and then the Czech national anthem, and was so moved that he decided that he would die too. But as he went inside the chamber a woman said to him: 'So you want to die? But that's senseless. Your death won't give us back our lives. That's no way. You must get out of here alive, you must bear witness to our suffering and to the injustice done to us.'

He survived five waves of liquidations before being freed.

Such stories beggar credence, and there are many of them. They make *Shoah* one of the most incredible acts of witness ever made – a terrible film that, in often matter-of-fact tones, makes the anti-history of David Irving shrivel. Strangely, the quieter it gets, the more it resonates in the mind. *Shoah*, once seen, doesn't bear thinking about. But think about it you do.

CLOSELY OBSERVED TRAINS

Directed by Jiri Menzel
With Vaclav Neckar, Jitka Bendova
Czechoslovakia, 1966, 92 minutes

Few European films are so affectionately remembered as *Closely Observed Trains*, one of the pinnacles of the Czech New Wave of the sixties, brutally cut short by the Soviet invasion of Czechoslovakia in August 1968, causing Milos Forman, one of its chief exponents, to flee to America. Jiri Menzel, the film's director, stayed, and was unable to make films for some time. *Closely Observed Trains*, however, won Hollywood's Best Foreign Language film, and the whole world was able to see it.

When, years later, he was eventually allowed to make a comparatively anodyne come-back feature, I interviewed him in London together with a translator who turned out to be a political minder. This was why every time I asked Menzel an even vaguely provocative question he kicked me gently under the table. It was a bit like a scene from *Trains* itself.

Menzel at his best is a superb miniaturist, equally at home on stage or screen, which was perhaps why he made such a good job of Bohumil Hrabal's book. It was not easy, since Hrabal's short stories are often based on multi-layered monologues within which language was all important. He had to translate all this into visual form and a more linear framework with the assistance of the author himself. He succeeded magically.

The film was shot in and around the Bohemian train station of Lodenice and set near the end of the Second World War. The central character is a shy young clerk with a putative love life he can't manage but otherwise no other serious problems. Nor apparently have any of the others who work at the station. But the triumph of the film is to show us that our petty destinies are inextricably linked to bigger events outside our lives, and that we can never escape from them.

That he does this with such tenderness, charm and guile, as well as producing an extremely funny film, is a measure of the longevity of the film's appeal. It was once thought by its detractors that the film lacked real bite. Some Marxists in the West called it bourgeois. But running through it is a desperate seriousness which hardly precludes politics. 'In my opinion, the true poetry of this movie, if it has any, lies not in the absurd situations themselves,' Menzel has said, 'but in their juxtaposition with obscenity and tragedy'.

To recount the details of the plot hardly gives more than a flavour of this much-loved film. A visiting Nazi controller explains to those at the station how, even in defeat, the Germans are triumphant, while the clerk's first experience of a bombardment and his sight of dead people on a passing train remind one of the war raging outside this little microcosm of the world. But the often absurd everyday life at the station provides a counterpoint to that. You could say that Menzel's love of small detail and his tenderness towards his characters leaves in almost everything your average Hollywood editor would cut. The result is what one can only describe as quietly uproarious.

Sexually, the film is not what one might call politically correct, and it is the quirky erotic episodes that so many remember – notably the moment when the randy young station guard, whom the clerk watches with increasing envy, rubber-stamps the bare backside of a flirtatious peasant girl he has contrived to spread across his lap.

The sequence of the clerk's eventual losing of his virginity to a very willing partisan girl is as closely observed as the trains themselves. Thus emboldened, he makes another date with the conductress, with whom he has already failed in bed, and goes off to sabotage a German ammunition convoy. He succeeds, but dies in the process.

Menzel, a very special talent whose work was later blunted by the self-consciousness his fame brought him, and who could never have gone to Hollywood to produce something as bold as Forman's *One Flew Over The Cuckoo's Nest* or *Amadeus*, later made the equally good and even more nostalgic *Capricious Summer* before being forced into a long silence. With these two films, however, he made a reputation which comfortably survived the greyness of Czech production in the censored seventies. It will last for a very long time as humanist cinema at its best.

THE TIME TO LIVE AND THE TIME TO DIE

Directed by Hou Hsiao-hsien
With You Anshun, Tian Feng, Mei Fang
Taiwan, 1985, 137 minutes

If the Taiwanese director Hou Hsiao-hsien hailed from a country like France, he would undoubtedly be more widely known as one of the world's foremost film-makers. Even so, his films have extraordinary currency on the film-festival circuit, and have received top prizes at Venice, Cannes and Berlin, the three major European festivals. They have also been shown in art houses in at least 40 countries. He's a major voice who has to pitch it pretty loud to be heard above the clamour of more commercial talents.

In a way this is his own fault since, after making two or three superbly attractive early films, he became as interested not only in the political and social intricacies of Taiwanese history which aren't exactly a turn-on for those in the West, but in new and complicated narrative forms. This made his work more difficult to penetrate, even for his own countrymen. Despite that, *The Flowers of Shanghai*, the last film of his that was presented at Cannes, was described by Richard Williams, who succeeded me as the *Guardian's* weekly reviewer, as worth all the rest of the programme put together.

The Time to Live and the Time to Die, a terrible English title (possibly based on the Douglas Sirk film which substituted 'love' for 'live' and an 'a' for 'the') was his second film to reach the West after the charming *A Summer at Grandpa's* and, like that film, was semi-autobiographical. In 1947, a man and his family leave the Chinese mainland and settle in a village in Taiwan. When the revolution comes, they decide to remain. The film spans several years of their life, recalled through the childhood of Ah-Ha-Gu, probably at least partly Hou himself.

The style of this family saga is spare and simple, but eloquence itself. Dotty old Grandma walks down a winding road, thinking she will soon reach her old home in China, the boy grows older and instead of playing marbles and listening to stories of the old days becomes a young man trying to prove himself on the streets. There are several sequences of amazing emotional power, such as the moment when the young man's father dies and he walks into the room, completely devastated by his first meeting with death.

The honesty and truth of this and other similar passages manages to summon up this little microcosm of the world perfectly. And that world

succeeds in reflecting the larger universe outside in the same way as Satyajit Ray's *Apu* stories did. Everything is right – the miraculous use of sound, the limpid cinematography, the natural acting create an atmosphere you can't forget.

People have often compared the earlier Hou to Ray and also to Ozu. But he has always claimed never to have seen the work of those directors, at least not at the time. Perhaps it is simply that great film-makers tend to think alike. The fact is, however, that he is very much his own man, ploughing a pretty lonely furrow, even in Taiwan. But after *City of Sadness* won the Golden Lion at Venice, the Taiwanese government began to regard him as their blue-riband director, despite seldom understanding his pictures, and sometimes objecting to their clear-eyed political content.

Hou went on to make more audaciously structured films like the masterly *The Puppetmaster*, the true story of a famous old folk artist. And *Flowers from Shanghai* was certainly one of the most visually satisfying you could wish to see. But his style is more minimalist now and more introspective. *A Time to Live* is perhaps one of his simplest most evocative films, and it's also one of his most universal in human terms.

THE SCARLET EMPRESS

Directed by Josef von Sternberg
With Marlene Dietrich, John Lodge, Louise Dresser
USA, 1934, 110 minutes

'The hallmark of camp is the spirit of extravagance. Camp is a woman walking around in a dress made of three million feathers... Camp is the outrageous aestheticism of Sternberg's six American movies with Dietrich' – Susan Sontag.

If you read Josef von Sternberg's *Fun in a Chinese Laundry*, a vastly entertaining autobiography that was also the justification of a career in Hollywood that ended in disaster, even though it produced a series of epics the like of which had never been seen before, you would think the director a control freak to end all control freaks.

For instance, he insists that in all the famous seven films he and Marlene Dietrich made together, every gesture, every expression and every movement was created by him. She was merely the little German puppet who photographed superbly and became a star by playing his tune. It wasn't quite true, though she never had the same feeling for any of her other directors.

But in *The Scarlet Empress*, my favourite of his films, it is certainly fact that he not only orchestrated the score, with bows to Tchaikovsky, Mendelssohn and Wagner, but conducted it as well.

Sontag was right in essence about camp, but even so I am quite prepared to accept *The Scarlet Empress* as great cinema since it was so much more than that. He was the master of light and shade, and of the kind of ancillary detail that might have seemed over-elaborate in other hands but in his contributed coherently to the whole.

He once said that he wouldn't mind showing his films upside-down, because their justification was not the story, nor the screenplay nor the acting, but 'the phenomenon of visual style'. You could say that he wrote with the camera, and that he often achieved poetry.

The Scarlet Empress can certainly be termed the work of a visual poet. And though no one would claim this tale of Catherine the Great, child and woman, is historically accurate – not even the Sternberg who claimed Catherine's private diary as authority – it was a mixture of legend and romance and fairytale that left camp far behind.

In the film, nothing is quite what it seems, both to Catherine and to us. Her kindly doctor turns out to be also the public hangman, and innocent little Catherine says: 'Can I become a hangman some day?' Whereupon he reads her a book about terrible tortures which Sternberg illustrates as if turning the pages of a book.

In the last image, the hangman pulls on a bell-rope, and the clapper is a naked man, dangling by his feet. It is clear that young Catherine is inheriting a world in which she will have to become 'the Messalina of the North' just to survive her mother's ambitions for her.

The film is full of Sternberg's obsessive, and often malicious, melancholy. There seems to be nothing in this world that is not corruptible as Catherine's fate pursues her, making her ambition fruitless and her attempts at love impossible. No matter how banal the dialogue, there is a constant sense that Sternberg's purpose isn't just to tell a story but to decorate it so that its meaning becomes crystal clear.

Of course Dietrich looks superb, as she always did for Sternberg, who knew he had found someone the camera loved. It was indeed what he called 'a dramatic encounter with light', illustrating the life and times of a woman who had to become ruthless, even compared to the men around her.

Some think the film an allegory about Hollywood – about a woman groomed for stardom by her mother, given a new image, presented to the public, pursuing power on her own account and finally dehumanised, imprisoned by her own image. And by associating Catherine with a white horse, Sternberg may have had in mind the legend of her death, attempting intercourse with a stallion.

But this is mere conjecture. The film remains, like all Sternberg's best work, beautiful, ironic, disturbing and erotic. And that is rather more than camp. Actually, it made the rest of Hollywood look camp, or at least banal.

SULLIVAN'S TRAVELS

Directed by Preston Sturges
With Joel McCrea, Veronica Lake
USA, 1942, 90 minutes

Preston Sturges once invented a kiss-proof lipstick, but he didn't stay in cosmetics for long, and it isn't entirely illogical that he eventually gravitated to Hollywood, at first as a scriptwriter and then as a writer-director the like of which we haven't really seen since.

He was a kind of well-connected anarchist within a system which frowned on such feelings, unless, that is, the result made money. People like Billy Wilder owed a great debt to him.

His America was cheerfully corrupt, wholly absurd and frequently unaware of its own ridiculousness, and his films were so high on energy and comic dynamism that you could readily forgive a certain detachment and a rather wayward lip-service to logic. In *The Great McGinty* (his first film as director in 1940), for instance, someone says that if it wasn't for graft you'd get a very low type of person in politics. Mere jellyfish, in fact. No wonder Hollywood often suspected him, as did the censors, since this was the period in which you were supposed to be patriotic. He was also called a cynic and a snob.

His glory days as a film-maker, however, were brief. Before the end of the decade he was worn out, and he died bankrupt and more or less forgotten in New York's Algonquin Hotel in 1959. During the forties, however, he made half a dozen comedies as subversive as any now and a good deal funnier. *Sullivan's Travels* is probably his masterpiece, but *The Miracle of Morgan's Creek, The Palm Beach Story,* or *Hail the Conquering Hero* would do as well.

Sullivan's Travels starts with Joel McCrea's Sullivan, a director of comedies who wants to get serious with an adaptation of a novel called *Brother, Where Art Thou?* being berated by studio bosses because he isn't making *Ants in their Pants,* and anyway doesn't know the meaning of the poverty the book talks about.

So he borrows a tramp's outfit from the wardrobe department and takes to the highway, with a large bus owned by the studio full of doctors, bodyguards and secretaries at a discreet distance behind him. The more he tries to break away from Hollywood, the faster it comes towards him. After picking up a failed actress who says things like 'There's nothing like a deep-dish movie for driving you out into the open', the rich man's search for poverty ends in a fight with a policeman which lands him in a Southern chain-gang.

In a key scene, he and the other convicts go to a black church hall where the minister instructs his already pretty unfortunate congregation to welcome those even less fortunate. And together everyone roars with laughter at a Disney cartoon. Sullivan may not have found seriousness, but at last he has found how valuable true comedy is.

Unconvincing as this may seem – and certainly sentimental – it is an unforgettable moment, perhaps telling us that the high art Sturges always despised is worthless if merely inspired by middle-class guilt. But even if you don't appreciate this defining sequence in the film, everything else gels perfectly. The ridiculous studio bus full of hangers-on trying to get Sullivan out of the scrapes he falls into, the butlers who strongly object to the whole enterprise, the ghastly wife who thinks he's dead and lays flowers on his supposed grave like a fashionable zombie.

Is the film serious underneath its hilarity? Perhaps not entirely, since Sturges never quite knew how to do it, like Sullivan himself. But the way the vast assemblage of characters who populate his films so magnificently so often seem to realise their own failings at least betokens a sophisticated, perhaps kindly cynic.

Sullivan's Travels is a hoot, but it is not quite just that, despite its brilliant mixture of visual gags that might have come from silent comedy and laughter generated by witty dialogue. People have tended to say that Sturges's films were as schizophrenic as he was. If that's so, long live abstracted directors, since they tend to see the world as it is rather than as we might wish it to be.

L'ATALANTE

Directed by Jean Vigo
With Michel Simon, Jean Daste, Dita Parlo
France, 1934, 89 minutes

It wouldn't seem possible, however eccentric the compiler, to compose a list of 100 films through which the cinema should be celebrated without including a work by Jean Vigo. Yet he made only four, short enough to be seen in one evening, and died of tuberculosis aged twenty-nine in 1934.

The last and greatest was *L'Atalante*, butchered for commercial release and, though partially restored, even now unable to be seen exactly as its director intended. He was the epitome of the radical, passionate film-maker who has to fight every step of the way against people of less imagination and sensibility – 'I'm willing to sweep up the stars' crap,' he once wrote when trying for a job as an assistant.

In the end, none of his films prospered until long after his death. But think of Renoir and of Buñuel, put the two together, and you have Jean Vigo – the son of a militant anarchist who had taken the name of Almereyda because it contained all the letters of 'merde' ('shit'), and was almost certainly murdered in prison.

L'Atalante was originally a simplistic story assigned to Vigo by Gaumont despite the fact that *Zero de Conduite*, his astonishing evocation of an unhappy childhood, had been banned by the censors. He changed it utterly, at least in tone, but had by then become so ill that he constantly risked collapse as he was making it. There is, however, no sign whatever of his impending death in the film itself.

L'Atalante is a barge in which a young newly married couple travel the waterways of France. The crew consists of an old eccentric with a passion for cats and a no less peculiar boy. Soon, the wife, though she loves her husband, grows tired of his waterbound obsessions and, longing for the excitement of Paris, is inveigled ashore by a pedlar.

Totally distraught, the young husband imagines he sees his wife reflected in the water. Meanwhile, she tires of wandering the cruel and

poverty-stricken Paris of the Depression years. There are prostitutes and beggars and thieves everywhere. Men try to pick her up, she has her handbag stolen, and goes forlornly in search of the barge. In the end, she is found by the old man, and the lovers are reunited.

The film is a masterpiece not because of the tragic story of its maker, nor because of its awkward genesis, but because, as Truffaut has said, in filming prosaic words and acts, he effortlessly achieved poetry.

The beginnings of the inarticulate young couple's life together has an erotic charge rare in the French cinema of the time. So have the sequences when, parted by their quarrel, they long for each other in silence. Vigo, said André Bazin, the French critic, had an almost obscene taste for the flesh. Consequently the couple's final reconciliation is the stronger and more moving.

Added to that, Vigo created characters, like Michel Simon's bargeman with a cigarette hanging from his bellybutton at one point, who, though larger than life, seemed absolutely true to it. This alone is an amazing performance. But then Simon was one of the greatest of screen presences. Vigo was not afraid of going beyond realism while still insisting on the grittiness of ordinary life.

The poetic power of the film, however, had a lot to do with the cinematography of the Russian-born Boris Kaufman, who worked on each of

Vigo's films and was said to be the youngest brother of the great Russian Dziga Vertov, and a collaborator with him on the famous Kino-Pravda films.

Kaufman later went to Hollywood, where *On The Waterfront* was one of his films, but he always recalled the days of working so closely with Vigo as 'cinematic paradise'. The images he and Vigo created with *L'Atalante* were dreamlike but intense, and entirely without sentiment. You have to think of the painter Corot. And the final shot of the barge, taken from on high, is an abiding triumph. Maurice Jaubert's superb score was a perfect match.

Gaumont found the film commercially worthless, hacked it to pieces and retitled it *Le chaland qui passe* (*The Passing Barge*), inserting a popular song of that name into the sound-track. It was advertised as 'a film inspired by the celebrated song so admirably song by Lys Gauty'.

Only a few days after the first disappointing run ended, Vigo died. His much-loved wife Lydou, lying beside him, got up from the bed and ran down a long corridor to a room at the end of it. Friends caught her as she was about to jump out of the window.

RAISE THE RED LANTERN

Directed by Zhang Yimou
With Gong Li, Ma Jingwu
China, 1991, 125 minutes

Until the so-called Fifth Generation of film-makers came along, most people thought of the Chinese cinema in terms of strident propaganda films like *The Red Detachment of Women*. In fact, China's film industry has been going for a great deal longer than most Westerners would imagine. Superb films like Xie Jin's *Two Stage Sisters*, a work some have compared to the best of Hollywood in both style and content, were produced some time before, and though Chen Kaige, Zhang Yimou and others seemed to be making a fresh start after the Cultural Revolution, they owed a debt to many others.

That said, their arrival gave China a massive presence at the film festivals of the world, even when the government was highly uncertain as to whether it liked the work of those who came to be the 'young Turks' of the Chinese cinema. And no film had a more startling effect on Western eyes than Yimou's *Raise the Red Lantern*, which rushed Gong Li, then its director's partner, and a star after *Red Sorghum* and *Ju Dou*, into the super-star league.

The film is set in the Northern China of the twenties, and Gong Li plays a young student who agrees, against the advice of her step-mother, who wants her to continue studying, to become the fourth wife of an ageing clan leader. Only nineteen, she finds herself confined to the old man's palatial complex, where his other three wives conspire with his courtiers and intrigue is permanently in the air. The red lanterns of the title are hung outside the rooms of whichever wife the clan leader presently favours, and it is soon clear that the only way the youngest one can compete is to provide good sex and then feign pregnancy.

Soon her power increases, since she is very beautiful and not as innocent as we think, but the intrigues of the other women and her own descent into paranoia lead inevitably to violence and tragedy. Yimou shot the film so that its rich colours and claustrophobic atmosphere matched the story perfectly, and he clearly gives it another dimension – that of a parable about the patriarchal, semi-feudal society of China itself. What's more, he took the audacious step of never showing us the old man himself, so that he remains a mysterious non-presence until the end.

The film was criticised in some quarters for trying to appeal with its exoticism as much to Westerners as to the people of Yimou's own country, and it was not approved of officially, even though one doubts whether the nervous government bureaucrats took its meaning correctly. But it remains a marvellously structured, richly imagined and extremely well acted piece of work, with a central performance that holds the attention from start to finish.

It is perhaps Yimou's most lavish and stately film, quite unlike his previous or following work in style. It is also his most resonant. You have only got to watch Gong Li being prepared for the marital bed to see how the film brilliantly captures the scent of sex, jealousy and impending disaster.

Yimou, who started as a cinematographer, and shot *Yellow Earth* for Chen Kaige – the film about the adventures of a Communist soldier visiting a backward village in 1939, which was to become the first major success for the Fifth Generation – is capable of many different styles. *Red Sorghum* might have been a western, and *Ju Dou* could have starred someone like Edward G. Robinson, while later *The Story of Qui Ju* had a touch of Ken Loach about it.

But he remains a master of story-telling with a distinctive ability to ally the personal to the political. If he has recently softened his approach, seemingly to curry favour with the authorities, he seldom fails to spike his tales with some criticism and a sharp eye for official hypocrisies.

McCABE AND MRS MILLER

Directed by Robert Altman
With Warren Beatty, Julie Christie
USA, 1971, 120 minutes

A critic has shrewdly commented that a great many westerns can be roughly divided into Democrat or Republican variants of the genre – Zimmerman's liberal *High Noon* and *Rio Bravo*, Hawks's riposte to that film, being obvious examples. But there are some which manage to transcend such considerations. Robert Altman's *McCabe and Mrs Miller* – one of the three best films he ever made in my opinion – is surely an example. It's like no other western I've seen.

For one thing, Altman's heroes are hardly the stuff of western legend. One (Warren Beatty) is a rather seedy pimp-cum-entrepreneur who rides into the shell of a small frontier town determined, somehow or other, to get rich. The other is a tough Cockney girl (Julie Christie) who convinces him that if he wants to start something like a brothel he ought to have a competent manager of women. Which is her.

These two are very human characters, nothing like as confident as they would have us believe. The actors playing them, as often happens in Altman pictures, seem to subsume their star personalities in a way most well-known faces in westerns signally fail to do. And surrounding them is a town growing up before our eyes as a wet autumn progresses into a cold winter.

It's the kind of movie that eavesdrops not just on its cast but on the grocery stores, the saloons, the brothels and the weather too. One critic has said that the camera is so unobtrusive that you feel everybody continues their conversations long after the camera is turned away from them. This, of course, is Altman's great strength. But he has seldom employed it with more discipline, though to say the film is beautifully staged somehow betrays his methods.

What the pair of potential misfits want is to get out of this canvas-tented dump and back to San Francisco, where the real money, and the real con artists are. But then, just as it looks as if they'll eventually make it, the enforcers come to town. They are prepared to kill people who won't sell out to the mining company, and their first victim, murdered on the suspension bridge that leads across the river to the general store, is a nice kid who means no harm to anyone. It's a superb sequence, and it tells you everything.

Later, as the church burns during an eerie snowstorm and the towns-people try to save it, McCabe finally gets his comeuppance, with his lover

back in Chinatown puffing opium. He sits dead on a snow-bank, almost as if reflecting how money and greed have finally undone him. That's what the film's about – the fact that almost everyone's on the make but the bigger fish eat the smaller.

America, Altman once told me, puffing at a cigarette that certainly wasn't tobacco, has been like that from the beginning, and it will remain that way for the forseeable future. The West was built by crooks, not the patriotic pioneers let loose upon it. Yet this is not a cynical film, though it certainly is ironic. It manages to be romantic and deadly at the same time.

I wrote at the beginning that this beautiful and oddly affecting film is one of the three best Altman movies. The others are *Nashville*, which is not so much about the state of the union at the time, as some say, but a near-perfect summation of a certain strata of American society in decline, and the relatively unknown *Tanner '88*, a long television satire, shot during the presidential campaign of that year, that tells us more about the absurdities of American politics than we would comfortably wish to know. At his best, Altman is a treasure we should cherish, warts and all. Even at his weakest, he's worth watching.

A SHORT FILM ABOUT KILLING

Directed by Krzysztof Kieslowski
With Miroslaw Baka, Krzysztof Globisz
Poland, 1987, 85 minutes

No European director of recent years, not even Pedro Almodovar, has been as much admired, at least by critics, as Krzysztof Kieslowski. Yet he had to wait many years for recognition outside Poland. The films that finally brought him into prominence were the ten called 'The Decalogue', loose commentaries on the ten commandments, originally made for Polish television. Each hour-long film was set within the same Warsaw suburb, and the whole project took only 18 months to shoot. Two of them were extended by Kieslowski into full-length features – *A Short Film About Killing* and *A Short Film About Love*. They illustrated 'Thou shalt not kill' and 'Thou shalt not commit adultery', and either would be candidates for my 100 best list.

I choose *Killing* because of the furore it caused in some circles. In Poland, the film was largely instrumental in the abolition of the death penalty. But not everybody admired it. At Cannes it received only the minor Jury Prize, and when it came to be considered for the short-list from which the first European Film Award was to be selected one juror called it a second-rate copy of an American film. Another said that it should be banned outright.

Only myself and Henning Carlsen, the Danish director, supported it, and the rest of the committee bowed to us by suggesting we could give it one nomination. We chose Best Film – a choice of which its opponents approved, thinking it would have no chance of that award with the final jury. To everyone's surprise, Kieslowski won.

The film is not an easy one to watch, being the story of a lumpen young man who bludgeons a taxi driver to death and is then caught, brought to trial, condemned to death and executed. Both deaths are dreadful, and Kieslowski is clearly trying to tell us that the one is as morally and physically repugnant as the other. The taxi driver is battered to death with a stone and takes some time to die, while the long-winded bureaucratic precision of the hanging was apparently so horrendous to film that Kieslowski's team had to break off in the middle.

It should be emphasised, though, that Kieslowski's two most violent scenes are not lingered over unduly. We see neither too little nor too much. They are certainly there to shock us, but for a good reason. What makes them so powerful is actually the rest of the film. It is shot by Slawomir Idziak with the aid of lowering, ochre-coloured filters that render the young man's world almost like a purgatorial nightmare. Never has Warsaw and its environs looked so depressing.

Added to that, we find out that the murderer has come from a bad home, and his lack of education is palpable. He cannot tell his defending counsel much upon which to launch a plea for mercy. He is a pathetic figure who, even if he had never killed, would seem set for a life of tragedy. Not for a moment does the film let us off the hook, and the atmosphere it creates and sustains is one of the most menacing I've encountered.

Most considering the work of this outstanding director, whose own favourite film-maker was Ken Loach – 'I'd happily work as a teaboy on one of his sets' – would probably choose a film not from the extraordinary 'Decalogue' but from the later 'Three Colours Trilogy', made largely in France. Brilliant as these latter films are, there is a case that his style became too refined, sometimes dominating the content. While it is almost impossible to conceive of Kieslowski ever making a bad film, in 'The Decalogue', and particularly in *Killing*, style and content were perfectly matched.

In an era when there are few genuinely great European directors left to us, his early demise was a terrible tragedy.

WELFARE

Directed by Frederick Wiseman
USA, 1975, 167 minutes

If ever a documentarist could be said to be objective, it is Frederick Wiseman who, for over 30 years now, has trained his camera on American life and institutions, having no obvious polemical stance but merely observing, sometimes in minute detail, what he finds. He shoots for many hours, so that his subjects begin to ignore the camera. But then he edits the collected material for much longer.

That process can't be objective, and he doesn't pretend it is. The surprise is that what he finds is often nothing like what we, or even he, might expect. Some have criticised his implicit even-handedness, remembering *Titicut Follies*, his first effort, about life in a prison for the criminally insane, which became mired in litigation with the state authorities and gave Wiseman the reputation of a controversial attacker of the system.

Thereafter, his films went less obvious ways. They neither courted notoriety nor sought to confirm or even deny expectations. Partially because of this, his body of work is of great and increasing value, almost as slices of the times we live in or, as he has called it, 'a form of natural history'.

One of his major works, and perhaps his masterpiece, is *Welfare*, which looks at the welfare system in New York from the points of view of both the officials administering it and the claimants who crowd their offices.

The result is both mind-boggling and eye-opening. Mind-boggling because this is clearly a bureaucracy pitted against people least fit to deal with it, and thus in essence inhuman. Eye-opening because, in spite of that, those running it are clearly not inhuman, and frequently go out of their way to accommodate those with lives so hopelessly muddled that it seems almost impossible to help them within the obtaining rules and regulations.

Any half hour of a long film provides revelations, like the girl claimant who's been told by the official who interviewed her that he's trying to look after two and a half million people, and that if a couple of thousand don't get what's due to them he's doing a very good job. Or the German immigrant on the skids who says God only helps you if he wants to, and that under the circumstances 'I think I'd better look for a nice place to hang myself'.

'Are you attending a clinic?' an officer asks a woman who says she's been ill. 'No'. 'Why not?' 'Because I have no money,' comes the utterly logical riposte. And without a note from a doctor, she can't get a dollar. An ex-druggie who got himself work, an apartment and a dog, but lost everything but the dog, is told he can have a room in a hostel. He objects that he can't take his dog there. But the man says: 'We're giving assistance to you, not your dog'. He won't go. 'I don't say it's right,' says a man who admits stealing food, 'I say it's necessary... I'm waiting for something that will never come – justice'. Every small tragedy is a large one for some people.

Even the police who patrol the offices through which the deserving and the undeserving poor shuffle, sometimes from one queue to another one somewhere else, get involved. They are mostly black and there are racists about, but they keep their cool, even when told they breed like rabbits and will cause blood on the streets one day if they're not wiped out first.

Throughout all this, Wiseman's camera simply looks and records. It doesn't have to do anything else. It's the editing that's important. We may see everything through his eyes, but we are at liberty to form our own opinions. David Thomson, the film critic and historian, disdains Wiseman's neutrality, wishing him to be crazier and at any rate less guarded. We should, however, be grateful for his essential lack of bias. It's one way to get at some sort of truth.

THE WIND

Directed by Victor Sjöström
With Lillian Gish, Lars Hanson, Montagu Love, Dorothy Cumming
USA, 1927, 70 minutes

Bergman's choice of Victor Sjöström, then seventy-eight, to play Isak Borg in *Wild Strawberries* was partly his way of paying tribute to a film-maker whom he much admired and by whom he was deeply influenced. Sjöström made films both in Sweden and America and was one of the chief reasons for the pre-eminence of the Swedish cinema just after the First World War. Between 1917 and 1921 he made four films of such technical mastery and luminous power that it was only a matter of time before Hollywood lured him across the water.

These films, full of the almost masochistic obsessions of Swedish Protestantism, but also extremely beautiful in their depiction of the elemental forces of nature, caused Sjöström, together with his equally famous fellow director Mauritz Stiller, to be characterised as a gloomy Swede, even though he both acted in and made comedies too. And in America his three most famous works – *He Who Gets Slapped*, *The Scarlet Letter* and *The Wind* each deal with human suffering.

The Wind is almost certainly the best – a silent classic, revived in recent years by Kevin Brownlow with a Karl Davis score, which gave the great

Lillian Gish one of the finest parts of her career. Like Sjöström himself in
Wild Strawberries, Gish dominates the picture as a Southern belle who
leaves Virginia for Texas, where a hard and desperate pioneer life is to
await her. Even before she gets there, we know what the film is about.
'Man, puny but irresistible, encroaching forever on Nature's Fortresses',
announces a title, as the wind blows remorselessly across the desert landscape through which Gish's Letty Mason passes.

The Texan family, attracted by her delicacy as much as she is repelled by their coarseness, begins to realise that she will be a sexual threat until she marries. So she chooses the more presentable of her two cowpoke suitors, soon realises the situation is impossible, and is attracted to a seemingly more sophisticated stranger. He, however, rapes her and she accidentally kills him. She guiltily buries him, only to find that the wind erodes the grave to expose the hand of her victim for all to see.

All very melodramtic in essence. But then the silent cinema could stand more of that than the cinema of both sound and vision. Besides, Sjöström treats the inevitable clash between Letty and her new surroundings with considerable realism and detail, allowing Gish as much leeway as possible to develop her performance.

The entire film was shot in the Mojave Desert under conditions of great hardship and difficulty, and this was probably the first western that tried for truth as well as dramatic poetry. One of its masterstrokes, which looks far less self-conscious than any description of it may seem, is the moment when Letty hallucinates in terror at the sight of the partially buried body of her attacker and a white stallion appears in the dust-storm as an omen of doom.

The stallion could be either a stray from the herd being rounded up by her husband nearby or the ghost of the north wind that, according to Indian legend, lives in the clouds. It's an extraordinary image ending an extraordinary film which even measures up to *Greed*, von Stroheim's slaughtered masterwork of 1924.

Sjöström made other films in Hollywood, most of which, including *The Divine Woman* with Garbo, have been either destroyed or lost. He was one of the very first group of film-makers whose work convinced often sceptical critics, mostly trained in literature and the theatre, that the cinema was capable of being a fully-fledged art form. No one would deny that *The Wind* is a work of art, or cavil much after seeing it with the opinion of a French critic who said that Sjöström was capable of making 'the most beautiful films in the world'.

MAN OF THE WEST

Directed by Anthony Mann
With Gary Cooper, Julie London, Lee J. Cobb
USA, 1958, 100 minutes

When Anthony Mann died in 1967, he was planning a western version of *King Lear*, with the monarch's daughters translated into sons. This long-cherished project might have been a classic, since no director of westerns made them nearer to classical tragedy, combining that with a feeling for landscape that equalled Ford. A critic has rightly said that they 'revel in the beauty of daylight, space and distance'. But the best of them also reveal in their often heroic protagonists an acute sense of human fallibility and self-doubt.

Almost all the James Stewart westerns directed by Mann in the fifties, like *Winchester 73* and *The Man From Laramie*, not only gave the actor a new lease of life but remain outstanding within the genre. But the greatest of all, *Man of the West*, made in 1958, starred Gary Cooper. He was Link Jones, a reformed gunfighter – the link perhaps between the old West and the new – who is placed in a predicament which means that he has to betray his new-found pacifism by annihilating one by one the gang who used to be his comrades.

The film brings to the fore all Mann's preoccupations and knits them perfectly together within a mere 100 minutes of screen time. *Lear* is paralleled by the fact that Lee J. Cobb's leader of the gang regards Link as his favourite son and, before he realises what is happening, has welcomed him back into the fold with open arms.

Link is travelling from a community he has helped to build to Fort Worth to find a teacher for the newly organised school when the train is ambushed and robbed by his former colleagues. Stranded in the desert with a gambler and a showgirl, he is forced to return to the gang's old hideout for shelter. There he gets into a fight with one of his old friends that ends in him stripping the man of his clothes. They are both humiliated by the experience – the crook for obvious reasons, Link because he has had to resort to a violence he has come to hate. If he wants to save himself and his whole new life, he realises there is only one way to do it. He has to deny everything he now holds dear.

The finale is inevitable. It is Cooper versus Cobb, and one of them will surely die. Both actors give extraordinary performances. Cooper, in real life getting old and sick with the cancer that was to kill him three years later, makes one last successful effort to prove he could be a consummate screen actor as well as a star, and Cobb, playing a character who had genuine fondness for the ex-gunman, contributes a dignified performance that does not entirely preclude our sympathy. The two men are, after all, reflections of each other.

Throughout Mann's direction is immaculate, making Reginald Rose's clearly allegorical and sometimes forced screenplay seem even better than it is. Every line is made to pay, and all the time the landscape seems like a presence that lends the story a perfect backdrop, often more threatening than beautiful.

Mann's career started with low-budget thrillers, progressed to westerns, and ended with epics like *El Cid* and *The Fall of the Roman Empire* (both of which might just as well have been Middle-Eastern westerns). He never glorified violence but set it implacably within the context of his stories, which illustrated the emotional limitations of his characters and the nature of their predicaments. Without a doubt he was a film-maker who, at his best, could be compared to anyone in his matching of the power of images with a blunt version of psychological truth.

TRIUMPH OF THE WILL

Directed by Leni Riefenstahl
Germany, 1935, 120 minutes

It is difficult to feel much sympathy for Leni Riefenstahl, the German film-maker whose *Triumph of the Will* proclaimed the virtues of National Socialism to the world in 1935. But it is also difficult not to admit that the film, a record of the Nuremberg rally of the previous year, commissioned and named by Hitler, proclaimed her as one of the most astonishing talents of that era.

Whatever she says to the contrary, and she has been fighting for *Triumph* to be recognised as 'purely historical' ever since, the film is easily the most staggering illustration of how a warped political credo can be transformed into a quasi-mystical Wagnerian showpiece for propaganda purposes.

'The creative outline,' Riefenstahl wrote in her booklet, *The Final Form*, 'demands that one should... find a coherent way to fashion the film so that it seizes and carries the viewer from act to act, from impression to impression, in an ever more overwhelming crescendo'. That she did, giving us a terrifying example of how and why Hitler won the hearts and minds of so many millions of Germans.

If one hates to admit Riefenstahl's merits as a director, and many still do, *Triumph* is at the very least a masterpiece of cinematography and editing. There were 16 of the best German cameramen using 30 cameras, backed up by 29 newsreel men, in the crew of 172 who fashioned the film to her orders. In all, over 60 hours were shot and the material took five months to edit.

Even Goebbels, the weedy-looking Nazi propaganda minister, who disliked Riefenstahl as a domineering and decidedly unweedy-looking woman, preferring his propaganda in the fictional form of such virulent epics as Viet Harlan's *Jew Suss*, had to praise the result.

Curiously, the scene is set in much the same way as Eisenstein created enormous tension in *October* with the anticipated arrival of Lenin in Finland. There is a prologue without vision, like some Wagnerian overture, before titles read: 'On 5th September 1934, 20 years after the outbreak of the War, 16 years after the beginning of German suffering, 19 months after the beginning of Germany's rebirth... Adolf Hitler flew again to Nuremberg to review the columns of his faithful followers'.

Then, intercut, are two sequences – the Führer's aircraft flying through the clouds, casting its shadow on the city streets below, and the marching columns of those arriving to welcome him. A small girl presents Hitler with a bunch of flowers and a cat stops washing its paws to glance at the motorcade. We are shown Nuremberg at dawn and the spirit of German history in its magnificent architecture. The music is the hymn 'Awake! The dawn of day draws near' from Wagner's *The Master Singers of Nuremberg*.

Such a start heralds first the jolly camaraderie of the camp and then the rally itself, culminating in Hitler's speech about the Party as a religious order, lasting into the millennia to come.

The whole ought to be boring and predictable. But Riefenstahl's brilliant cutting, her striking sense of the visual, her use of darkness and light, and the often rhythmic movement of her cameras avoids the static newsreel style she so abhorred. It makes hideous sense of Hess's remark at its conclusion: 'The Party is Hitler. But Hitler is Germany, just as Germany is Hitler'.

Riefenstahl, striking enough to be a star in a whole series of pantheistic German mountain films, and also the director as well as star of *The Blue Light*, one of the most famous of them, went on to make three more films, one of them uncompleted, before forced into permanent silence by the fame, or infamy, of *Triumph of the Will*. But those interested in her extraordinary life should see Ray Muller's fascinating documentary, in which she still maintains her innocence of Fascism. It is appropriately called *The Wonderful Horrible Life of Leni Riefenstahl*.

BROADWAY DANNY ROSE

Directed by Woody Allen
With Woody Allen, Mia Farrow, Nick Apollo Forte
USA, 1984, 84 minutes

Despite the often cruel strictures of many American critics, who seem to think him a bore, I couldn't contemplate a list of favourite films without one from Woody Allen. He is, after all, one of the most fluent directors in America, and certainly a funnier man than Jim Carrey, Steve Martin or Adam Sandler.

But it may be thought a little eccentric to choose *Broadway Danny Rose* above the much-Oscared *Annie Hall*, or perhaps *Manhattan*. It is, however,

one of his most perfect films – a comedy about a legendary New York talent agent who gets hold of a washed-up crooner and propels him back into near-stardom. Allen plays Danny not as the usual Woody character, full of self-doubt, but as a minor wizard who could make a piano-playing bird into a genuine celebrity. Enthusiasm is his middle name.

Perhaps I like this film so much because of its lack of the ambition that besets Allen from time to time, causing the kind of hollow copy of Bergman that was *Interiors* or the cold proficiency of the admittedly very clever *Zelig*. Besides, it's incredibly true about the lower reaches of show-biz – always more fascinating than the higher echelons (which John Osborne realised when he wrote *The Entertainer*). And if you're the sort of person who wants to hear what the loser has to say rather than the winner, then either *Broadway Danny Rose* or *Radio Days* come high on the list of unselfconscious but most precisely observed Allen films.

Nick Apollo Forte is Lou Canova, a singer not of the first rank and also an alcoholic with a mistress who belongs to a Mafia hood as well as a long-suffering wife. He's so good in the part that you wonder what became of him, just as you wonder what becomes of Lou when Danny finally has to give up on him. He and Woody are the centre of gravity at this celebration of a Broadway not too far from Damon Runyon. Around them are spread the out-of-work no-hopers, the vicious and ungrateful success stories, the dumb showgirls and the even dumber gangsters we've come to know so well in lesser if much more portentous movies.

The film starts marvellously, with a group of comics sitting around a Carnegie Deli table trading stories about Danny and his exploits on behalf of his clients. And since Allen wrote the script, even the made-up ones are funny. Then we see how Danny gets Lou on the road again, riding the nostalgia boom of the time, booking him into Top Forty concerts and finally finding him a date at the Waldorf with Milton Berle in the audience looking for guests for his TV special.

Lou trying to persuade Danny to take his girlfriend to the Waldorf so she won't get upset is another hilarious sequence. But if he's good – a drunken egotist with a heart of silver if not gold – so is Mia Farrow as the girl, a brassy Mafia blonde with a taste in hair and dress styles that looks as if it might suit the fashion sense of a lowly henchman of Capone.

In all, this is a film which inhabits New York just as well as *Annie Hall* but looks at a different kind of instantly recognisable inhabitant. It sails near caricature perhaps at times. But then so does the world we're observing. As for Danny Rose himself, this is one of Woody's most actorly performances. For once he forgets himself and plays someone else. This isn't to downgrade his other good films. Just to say that sometimes small is best.

$8\frac{1}{2}$

Directed by Federico Fellini
With Marcello Mastroianni, Anouk Aimee, Sandra Milo, Claudia Cardinale
Italy, 1963, 140 minutes

At least half of all film-makers asked about the directors they most admire include Federico Fellini in their top three. And he seems to have a particular fascination for purely commercial directors – perhaps because his was the cinema of visually expressed emotions rather than intellectual rigour. He was indeed an exceptional director, warts and all. But there's a kind of critical resistance to his work which once caused him to write to me, then deputy critic for the *Guardian*, to see if there was anything I could do about the carping notices which invariably flowed from the pen of Richard Roud, my predecessor.

There was not. But I have to confess that the longer he worked, the more I doubted Fellini. In fact, my favourite of his films has always been his first – *Variety Lights*, which he co-directed with Alberto Lattuada way back in 1950. It's a marvellously sympathetic study of a travelling theatre group which, perhaps because I was once an actor, seems to me the best film about the theatre I've ever seen.

No doubt, however, that *8½*, made 12 years later, was his real masterpiece, *La Dolce Vita* and the *Fellini-Satyricon* his most spectacular epics, and *Amarcord* the self-referential one which turns his most faithful supporters weak at the knees.

8½ is probably the most potent movie about film-making, within which fantasy and reality are mixed without obfuscation and there's a tough argument inside the spectacle that belies Fellini's usual felicitous flaccidity.

Its title refers to the fact that, up to then, Fellini had made seven features and two episodes in composite films, adding up to about a half, and its central character is Guido (Marcello Mastroianni), a film-maker based at least partly on Fellini himself. He's a successful director with everything in place to make another hit, but no actual story to tell – perhaps as Fellini felt after the success of *La Dolce Vita*.

He procrastinates, retreats into his messy private life with wife and mistress, goes to a nightclub clairvoyant who makes him recall his childhood, and fantasises either about keeping a harem of women at bay with a whip or about being hounded to death by desperate producers and a hostile press. The only difference as far as autobiography is concerned is that Guido never makes his film, and Fellini did.

When it came out, the film seemed incomprehensible to many who had hitherto loved his work. In one Italian town, in fact, the audience attacked the projectionists for their part in showing it. As far as Fellini was concerned, however, the film was 'sincere to the point of being indecent' and not at all difficult to understand.

Later, critics referred to Jung, Kierkegaard, Proust, Gide, Pirandello, Bergman and Resnais in burrowing for his influences, and Alberto Moravia insisted that Guido was an Italian version of James Joyce's Leopold Bloom. Fellini strenuously denied he'd read any of these authors or seen any of the relevant films. But it's certainly true that many others were making subjective films at around the same time, notably Bergman (*The Silence*) and Kazan (*The Anatolian Smile*). 'Certain issues are in the air,' was all Fellini would say.

He won his third Oscar with *8½*, so it can hardly be as complicated as some have made out. But it does indeed remind one of Bergman, with whom Fellini was going to collaborate on a film, together with Kurosawa. Nothing came of it, but Fellini remembers meeting Bergman at Cinecitta, the great Roman studio within which he made so many of his films.

At one point, Bergman 'pointed with his very long finger to a corner of the swimming pool. Beneath the rain-rippled surface of the water an infinity of little organisms, like a Sumerian alphabet, were whirling around at bacterial velocity. Bergman squatted down on his heels and 'began talking to the tadpoles with a happy smile on his face'.

Both directors regard human beings slightly as if they were tadpoles, but whereas Bergman divorced himself from the equation, Fellini, at least in *8½*, did not. Which is why it is a better film even than *The Silence*.

APOCALYPSE NOW

Directed by Francis Coppola
With Martin Sheen, Robert Duvall, Marlon Brando
USA, 1979, 153 minutes

No war left so many scars upon the American psyche as Vietnam, not even the Civil War. And no film broke open those scars better than Francis Coppola's *Apocalypse Now*. In an interview, Coppola described his film as 'an experience that would give its audience a sense of the horror, the madness, the sensuousness and the moral dilemma of the Vietnam war'.

It was a grandiose project, culled indirectly by John Milius and Coppola from both Joseph Conrad's *Heart of Darkness* and from Michael Herr's *Dispatches*, and it took Coppola 238 days to shoot in the Philippines at more than double its original budget. By the end, almost everybody concerned was either sick or exhausted. But the result, though flawed, was undoubtedly one of the most resonant movies about war ever made, particularly unforgettable in its 70mm format, which is different from the 35mm version.

Not everyone would agree. One critic cleverly described it as a dumb movie that could only have been made by an intelligent and talented man. But if that is so, the dumbness reflected America's own attitude to the war, the effect of which has even now not been fully exorcised. *Apocalypse Now* will probably never be equalled as a metaphor for a whole nation's confused aspirations and the dogged obstinacy with which it pursued them.

Basically the film is a quest movie, but it moves through several other genres as well, such as thriller, horror, adventure and even comedy as Martin Sheen's Captain Willard searches for Marlon Brando's renegade Colonel Kurtz, who is waging a private war from a Cambodian temple near the Vietnam frontier. Kurtz's career must be terminated with extreme prejudice, as if the military-industrial complex basically responsible for the hostilities were some sort of Godfather-like Mafia sending a hitman to deal with a disloyal *capo*.

One remarkable sequence after another follows as Willard doggedly pursues his prey, many of them action sequences envisaged by Milius as he transposed Conrad from colonial Africa to Vietnam, but given a mythical, hallucinatory quality by Coppola and Vittorio Storaro, his lavishly brilliant cinematographer. Who can forget Robert Duvall's Colonel Kilgore and his helicopter cavalry zapping a waterfront village to the strains of Wagner's 'Ride of the Valkyries', broadcast over loudspeakers to scare the enemy? And who doesn't remember the line 'I love the smell of napalm in the morning'?

Storaro and Walter Murch, the film's sound editor, have perhaps their greatest moment at night when, after dropping acid, Sam Bottoms's boat crewman watches the Vietcong bombardment of an American-held bridge. We can't be sure that what he sees is affected by the drug or not as flames, smoke, flares, tracers and the shriek of shells illuminate the purgatorial darkness. Then there are the Playboy bunnies, helicoptered in to entertain the troops and forced to evacuate hurriedly when a riot threatens to engulf them.

Perhaps the Brando-dominated finale, with the actor frequently muttering almost incomprehensibly and the Angkor Wat-like temple seeming almost out of another movie, is the one area where the film flails too hard at mysticism to convince – Conrad dubbed into Hollywoodese. But even here, the intensity of Coppola's vision has a rivetting quality which prevents sneers.

Orson Welles almost made *Heart of Darkness* before he transferred his allegiance to *Citizen Kane*. It might have been an astonishing film. But not more so than Coppola's, which somehow manages to reflect with some accuracy what Conrad once wrote: 'It was like another art altogether. That sombre theme had to be given a sinsiter resonance, a tonality of its own, a continued vibration that, I hoped, would hang in the air and dwell in the ear after the last note had been struck.'

KIND HEARTS AND CORONETS

Directed by Robert Hamer
With Dennis Price, Alec Guinness, Joan Greenwood, Valerie Hobson
UK, 1949, 106 minutes

Of all those involved in the production of British films in the forties and fifties, Robert Hamer was possibly the most intelligent and talented. He was arguably Ealing Studios' brightest star, yet his career was shortlived and ultimately disastrous. He made his directing debut in 1945 and died largely unfullfilled at the age of fifty-two in 1963. His gradual descent

into alcoholism was one of the greatest tragedies of our cinema. But at least it could be said that he made one masterpiece. *Kind Hearts and Coronets* is not only one of the very best British films, but one of the most extraordinary black comedies the cinema has known.

To call it an Ealing comedy is really a misnomer. It has very little in common with the rest of the genre which, however entertaining and well-made, projected a view of Britain that was largely cosily fictitious – England, in particular, as we would like it to have been after the trauma of war. *Kind Hearts and Coronets* was much cooler, darker and more aware of sexual irony.

Hamer wanted to do three things. First, to make a film totally different to what had gone before, second, to use the English language in a more interesting way, and third, to pay as little regard as possible to the moral conventions of the time. People have said that his style was a combination of Wildean wit and the essential pessimism of such post-war French directors as Marcel Carné.

That he succeeded, in spite of working for the puritanical, narrow-gutted Michael Balcon, was a minor miracle. The other miracle was that the film was a success, making the reputation of Alec Guinness, confirming that of the now almost forgotten and certainly underrated Dennis Price, and reaching the status of a classic which could be viewed simply as a funny and clever entertainment if its more serious undertones were ignored.

It is revived so often that it seems hardly necessary to detail the plot, most of it told as a long flashback with attendant narration from the leading character. Price plays Louis Mancini, condemned to death for a murder of which he is innocent and writing his memoirs, about all those he has actually killed, in prison. His mother had been disowned by her proud aristocratic family for marrying an Italian singer and left to live in acute poverty.

At her graveside, Louis vows vengeance, and slowly but surely eliminates those who stand between him and the dukedom he doesn't particulary desire but is determined to claim for her sake. In achieving this he becomes as cold and calculating as the horrid d' Ascoyne family itself. But the major trick of the film, of course, is to have Guinness playing every one of them.

Guinness' performance is a tour de force. Nine characters in one film has to be, and most of them are a superb mixture of disguise and parodic vigour. But Price's bitter, sophisticated Louis ought not to be underestimated. A homosexual at a time when it was virtually impossible to admit it, at least in showbusiness, he put a whole slice of himself into his performance. It was almost as if both he and Robert Hamer had something to prove.

Hamer, in particular, worked against all the rules. He allowed the suppressed passion of the story full rein, getting pretty near a particularly English kind of eroticism at some moments. His ambiguous feelings about the family values Balcon always espoused were made patently clear. His sense of atmosphere, which burrowed surprisingly deep into the English subconscious, was maintained with brilliant strokes of his directorial pen. And all the time he let people laugh as if he was merely making a well-honed comedy.

It seems almost unbelievable that after his crowning achievement Hamer's career went consistently downhill. He was, said Balcon, 'engaged in a process of self-destruction'. But Balcon and others certainly helped him on his way. Perhaps *Kind Hearts and Coronets* was a giant fluke, able to get away with its subversion because it proved so popular. But there is little doubt that English good taste closed in on Hamer and on most of British cinema until the sixties reignited the element of revolt against it.

THE GENERAL

Directed by Buster Keaton and Clyde Bruckman
With Buster Keaton, Marian Mack
USA, 1926, 77 minutes

I remember once acting, as the Clown in *All's Well that Ends Well*, for the famous producer Neville Coghill. Dissatisfied with my somewhat feeble attempts to make my character funny in rehearsals, Coghill said to me kindly: 'Very good, Malcolm. But could you possibly do him as Buster Keaton?' 'No,' I replied, 'I don't think I'm up to that'. 'Okay,' said Coghill, 'Do Stan Laurel then'.

The thought that I could possibly emulate Keaton was a good deal more hilarious than the not very funny Shakespearean lines I had to utter, since there are a great many decent judges who think that Buster was the greatest clown in cinema history. He is now more fashionable than Chaplin, more loved than the Marx Brothers and – because of his sad, alcoholic decline, partly brought about by being sold into the unsympathetic hands of MGM – elevated into one of the tragic geniuses of the movies.

Undoubtedly Old Stoneface was a genius, both as a comedian who refused Chaplin's melodramatic pathos and as a director who was capable of making truly beautiful films if left to his own apparently somewhat haphazard devices. *The General* was such a movie, based on a true incident during the American Civil War when a posse of Northern soldiers hijacked a Confederate train and a lone Southern engineer found himself fighting the lot of them alone.

Keaton plays the engineer, turned down both for military service and by his silly girlfriend, who thinks he's a coward. When his engine is stolen by Northern spies, with her aboard, his pursuit has him crossing enemy lines, over-hearing the Unionists' secret plans, rescuing the girl, regaining the engine, beating off the enemy hordes, and returning to a huge welcome and an army commission. There's a large slice of luck in this, because Keaton never made a hero of his characters.

The plot is built around the central motif of the rail chase, which becomes an inexhaustible source of extremely elaborate comedy. But the gags are never there for their own sake and seem totally integral to the story. What's more, Keaton catches the essence of the Civil War period impeccably. It is a totally anti-heroic and anti-romantic film, turning all the cliches about the war on their heads and into comic bits and pieces.

Above all, *The General* seems like a film from a real director, almost perfect in structure and full of the rhythms of his best shorts. Unlike

Chaplin's, Keaton's films were outdoor movies, giving him the space to work and often vast panoramas to contrast with his moving body – 'that small piece of elastic granite' as a critic once called it. He was the little man juxtaposed against a huge universe, and he did all his stunts himself, playing against, in his various films, a dinosaur, an ocean liner, the entire Union and Confederate armies, the New York police force, Chinese crime wars, a tribe of Indians and a whole series of giant mechanical objects. Usually, what dwarfed him in the beginning became an ally he used to defeat his enemies at the end.

The General contains all the values of the Keaton canon, in which his sense of parody (*The Birth of a Nation* here) and irony are supreme. But it's the brilliance of the gags that make him unique. Behind the blank eyes and frozen face, which seldom if ever smiles, there was this ticking mechanism of a brain that could, in one stroke, make you laugh like a drain. He could also achieve acrobatics a circus performer would envy, culled from his time in vaudeville as a youth, when his father held his ankles and swept the stage with his hair. There was no one quite like Keaton, and there never will be.

LBJ AND OTHERS

Directed by Santiago Alvarez
Cuba, 1962, 18 minutes

If I were asked to recommend the perfect short to be studied by young film-makers, it would probably be the 18-minute *LBJ*. For the more impatient, it could be the six-minute *Now*. For those who need more, it might be either the 25-minute *79 Springs* or the 38-minute *Hanoi, Tuesday 13th*. They were all made by the same director – Santiago Alvarez of Cuba.

Alvarez, a committed son of Castro's revolution and a natural successor to the great Russian Dziga Vertov, would be classed as a documentarist if he hadn't always denied it. Instead, he called himself a news pamphleteer who, like Vertov, had to react to events as fast as possible since 'he who hits first, hits twice'.

His methodology as a socialist was to attempt to use images as powerfully as the West does to sell goods – 'the advertisements of capitalism are, in fact, much better than the product. The Jesuits were their precursors. Remember that saying about giving them a child. Remember too the famous old-style Coca Cola bottle. Why do you think it was designed like that? Feel it and you will find out. It is in the shape of a woman wearing the long dresses of the time. When a woman has a good body, we say in Cuba that she is Coca Cola.'

All the films I have mentioned are astonishing in their use of the image, always superbly underlined by music. *Now*, for instance, uses a song by Lena Horne which was banned in America but given to him for nothing by the singer for use in the film. A highly emotional commentary on racism, using mostly pirated newsreel images, it syncopates music and images with astonishing precision.

LBJ is a bitter satire on President Johnson, one of Alvarez's favourite targets, in three sections which correspond to Johnson's three initials. 'L' is for Martin Luther King, 'B' is for Bobby Kennedy and 'J' is for Jack Kennedy. Alvarez implicates Johnson in all three assassinations, portraying his presidency as the culmination of a whole history of socio-political corruption. Clips from Hollywood movies and a cartoon of Johnson as the all-American Texan cowboy are used as reinforcements.

Hanoi, Tuesday 13th is a moving celebration of Vietnamese culture and the country's courageous and long-standing battle for freedom from the Chinese, Japanese, French and Americans. *79 Springs* is a tribute to Ho Chi Minh (the title refers to his age at the time of his death). Both are equally remarkable – the latter being perhaps the most poetic film Alvarez ever made, constructing and deconstructing images with virtuoso brilliance.

At one point, a title which says 'Don't let disunity in the socialist camp darken the future' is torn to pieces, leaving the screen blank. Then a gunshot announces a split-screen, multi-image sequence of war and destruction, ending on a freeze frame which burns up to leave nothing. Finally the pieces of the title join up again and, to the music of Bach, bursts of gunfire flash across the screen before another title appears declaring that the Americans will be finally defeated.

Alvarez's polemic, of course, looks naive now at a time when it is fashionable to balance aggressive argument with so-called objective truth. Revolutionaries are well out of fashion.

But the point about Alvarez is not just his highly emotional commitment, which in itself is often surprisingly moving as well as effective. It is his amazing skill as a film-maker that hits the nerve-ends. 'Give me two photographs, a moviola and some music and I'll make you a film,' he once said, and he was true to his word, as the six-minute *Now* suggests.

Working quickly, often with practically nothing, and with equipment film-makers would reject as totally inadequate, he made a series of films in the sixties and early seventies which have yet to be beaten either as propaganda, or newsreels, or as pieces of brilliantly improvised cinema. Why have we forgotten him?

THE BAND WAGON

Directed by Vincente Minnelli
With Fred Astaire, Cyd Charisse, Jack Buchanan
USA, 1953, 111 minutes

Though it's patently true that the film musical reached its highest point of achievement in America, three of its most talented pioneers were from France, Germany and the Caucasus. They were René Clair, who never made a film in Hollywood, and Ernst Lubitsch and Reuben Mamoulian, who did. Each of these three could lay claim to early masterpieces of the genre. They, and especially Mamoulian, deserve to join Busby Berkeley, Vincente Minnelli and Stanley Donen as the most consistently brilliant directors of musicals.

I had a hard time deciding upon my choice from the work of this glorious six, but came down in favour of Minnelli's 1953 *The Band Wagon* for three reasons. The first was that it starred Fred Astaire, certainly one of the greatest dancers of the century in whatever medium, a very handy singer and an actor who somehow glided through his lines as if he was created to speak them.

The second was that it was produced, like most Minnelli musicals, by Arthur Freed, whose record at MGM was second to none in liberating the genre from the backlot and collecting an astonishing array of talent with which to widen its appeal. Besides, he wrote the lyrics for the title number of *Singin' in the Rain*. The third was that I happen to prefer my musicals inconsequential rather than serious or mock-serious. In other words, Mamoulian's underrated *The Gay Desperado* or *Silk Stockings* (which *Sight and Sound* had the temerity to call a 'vulgar and only rarely comic anti-Soviet tirade') to *Carmen Jones* or *West Side Story*.

The plot of *The Band Wagon* is totally inconsequential, though scenarists Betty Comden and Adolph Green have claimed the picture as a *film à clef*. Astaire, by then in his fifties, is an ageing star trying to make a come-back in a show written by his friends. A daftly portentous director (Britain's Jack Buchanan) teams him with a well known and haughty ballerina (Cyd Charisse), and the show is an unmitigated disaster. But as Astaire and Charisse move from dislike to attraction, they somehow manage to turn it into a hit.

Comden and Green say that Buchanan, trying to turn Goethe's *Faust* into a Broadway hit, is a spoof of Minnelli himself, sometimes inclined to pretention.

There will continue to be endless argument as to who was Astaire's best partner – Charisse, who could almost match him as a dancer, or Ginger

Rogers, of whom it is rightly said that she gave him sex appeal. One is perhaps fonder of Rogers, whose shoes were said to be sometimes full of blood after rehearsing with the meticulous Astaire, and who was certainly the better actress.

But Charisse, with the most elegant and eloquent legs in the business, was the same sort of total dancer as Astaire, and you have only to look at *Party Girl* to see the sensuousness behind the perhaps rather chilly if beautiful mask.

In *The Band Wagon* she did pretty well, and danced like an angel, thanks at least partly to choreography from Michael Kidd that, of its particular kind, has never been surpassed. Astaire's easy style and British star Jack Buchanan's ironic panache were a pretty good match.

Veteran composers Howard Deitz and Arthur Schwartz also produced a score that vies with the best, though it's scarcely believable that *That's Entertainment!* was written for the film in less than an hour.

But the whole point about *The Band Wagon*, and one which sometimes makes people underrate it, is the way everything seems to mesh so seamlessly – almost effortlessly, in fact. That was due to Minnelli, whose flair and imagination, admittedly aided by the huge array of MGM talent both behind and in front of the cameras, was matched by his almost perfect control.

Watching the best Minnelli films now, we are inclined to take this control for granted, as if he just had to throw the whole thing together with the appropriate craftsmanship and energy to keep us amused. But Minnelli's work was as precise as Astaire's, and that's what made him so fine a director. 'If you want to do a musical, it requires as much preparation as Hamlet,' he once said.

The Band Wagon was scarcely that, being more like one of Shakespeare's comedies, pushed up to date and set to music and dance, like Branagh's version of *Love's Labour's Lost*. But the more you look at it, the more perfect it seems. Hollywood doesn't make films like this now because public taste has changed. But it's doubtful if it could anyway.

Some people say, by the way, that the idea for the film was taken from the British radio show by Arthur Askey and Richard Murdoch. I'd be surprised, but if so, that seemed pretty good too in its day.

VIRIDIANA

Directed by Luis Buñuel
With Silvia Pinal, Fernando Rey, Francisco Rabal
Spain/Mexico, 1961, 90 minutes

A great many directors, when asked to name their favourite film-maker, invoke the name of Luis Buñuel. It isn't surprising, since he was undoubtedly a genius who had the invaluable capacity to offend and delight at the same time. You could choose any of a dozen of his films as one of the best 100. *Viridiana* is my choice, since it caused the maximum annoyance to people one is quite glad to see offended.

It was made in Spain in 1960 after Franco had told his Minister of Culture to invite the country's leading film-maker back from exile in Mexico to make whatever film he liked. But once he completed it, Buñuel sensibly decamped, perhaps deliberately leaving a few out-takes behind to be instantly burned by the authorities.

The film was, of course, banned outright in Spain and the Minister reprimanded for okaying the submitted script. But it won the Palme d'Or at Cannes, despite protests about it representing Spain and articles in the *l'Osservatore Romano*, the Vatican's official organ, saying it was an insult not just to Catholicism but to Christianity itself.

That was exactly what Buñuel intended. He had long ago lost his faith, and *Viridiana* was the score he had to settle with the Catholic Church, for its support of Franco and what he considered to be many other sins. 'I hope I don't go to hell,' he once said. 'Imagine the table talk of all those Popes and Cardinals.'

Viridiana, played by Silvia Pinal, is a novitiate about to take her final vows. She's so devout that she wears a crown of thorns and a large wooden crucifix over her simple shift in bed. Unfortunately her uncle (the great Spanish actor Fernando Rey) becomes hopelessly obsessed by her and gets his servant to drug her.

But seduction is beyond him, and he hangs himself after telling her he actually managed it. Bound to his estate by this fantastic turn of events, she invites a band of beggars to live there, hoping to reclaim them, and possibly herself, through prayer and charity.

They, however, have different ideas, and take over the house for a first-class orgy. One of them even rapes her. Totally disillusioned (like Buñuel), she plays a game of cards, to the strains of 'Shake Your Cares Away', with her uncle's illegitimate son and the servant who is his mistress. It looks as if some kind of *ménage-à-trois* is in the offing.

Sequence after sequence of this extraordinary film, incredibly Spanish but incredibly offensive to many Spaniards – especially the conservatives

who thought respectable women had no sexual urges – shows the simplicity of a master film-maker (sometimes aping the paintings of Goya) and the sophistication of a mind determined to play as many games as possible with his audience (echoing the writer Galdos).

The scene which has Viridiana piously collecting her beggars, each the ugliest or most deformed she can find, and their singing of the 'Angelus' as a rubbish truck thunders by drowning them out, is later contrasted with their ungrateful party in the lush villa. A leper is dressed as a bride and the company is suddenly frozen into a replica of da Vinci's 'The Last Supper' (to the crackling strains of Handel's 'Hallelujah Chorus' on the gramophone – which continues as she is molested).

This, suggests Buñuel, is what happens to saints – their virtues pay them back in pitch-black spades in a dire world. They can become martyrs if they wish, but their acceptance of things as they are is undoubtedly the best course.

People have said that Buñuel was first and foremost a Spaniard and then a surrealist, and it is no accident that the ending of *Viridiana* resembles that of *L'Age d'Or*, his great surrealist masterpiece made 30 years previously. But there's a bleak despair about this film which wasn't in that earlier work.

'I should like,' he once famously said, 'to make even the most ordinary spectator feel that he is not living in the best of all possible worlds'. The forces of darkness, he suggests, await us all. Perhaps he should have been on Prozac. But then we would never have had *Viridiana*, one of the great feel-bad movies of all time.

NIGHT OF THE HUNTER

Directed by Charles Laughton
With Robert Mitchum, Shelley Winters, Lillian Gish
USA, 1955, 93 minutes

Nothing could be more remarkable than the fact that an actor known for his vanity as well as his brilliance, who wanted to become a director largely because of the doubts he had about the merits of most of those with whom he worked, was capable of making a film like *Night of the Hunter*. But classic Charles Laughton's film is, encompassing one of the very best performances of Robert Mitchum's career as the murderous Preacher Powell.

A commercial, if not entirely a critical, failure, the public reception of it ensured that Laughton was never asked to direct again. Now, however, this 1955 film looks better and better – much more than the 'nightmarish sort of Mother Goose tale' which Laughton called it. It's also a complex study of good and evil, innocence and betrayal, though it did indeed have a dream-like quality. But it also had the strength and power of the best tales of E.T.A. Hoffmann.

The protagonists are children remorselessly pursued by an evil, hymn-spouting stranger who, having murdered their mother (Shelley Winters), seeks to steal from and kill them too. One of them at least knows that the word 'hate', written on the fingers of the preacher's left hand, is more appropriate than the word 'love' tattoed on his right.

But we, like the adults, are less certain that they are right to run away down the river into the Mississippi swamplands. This is, after all, Robert Mitchum and he can't be all that bad, can he? In the end he is, and they are saved only by the appearance of the fairy godmother figure of Lillian Gish's spinster Rachel, the Christian protector of strays, whether children or animals.

This is a moral film that nevertheless gives us a tantalising glimpse of something akin to purgatory. It's far more frightening than all but the best horror films, though it defies the genre tag, whether as thriller, horror or allegory.

It is easier to see how Laughton, a superb performer himself, got such a devastating portrait out of Mitchum, than how he managed to make the whole so satisfying as an entity. But he did have a good team behind him, which even he grudgingly recognised.

Stanley Cortez was one of the last great black-and-white cinematographers, who shot Welles's *The Magnificent Ambersons* and here sought and got an extraordinary atmosphere of menace, mixed with the naked beauty of the Deep South during the Depression years. Walter Schumann's music is exceptional too. But Laughton had to make the choices, and he did so with unerring skill.

He was generous about Mitchum, as almost everybody who directed him was, despite the star's celebrated put-down of himself – 'Paint my eyes on my eyelids, man, and I'll walk through it'. Laughton called him 'one of the best actors in the world, a tender man and a great gentleman'. And if you want to see the worth of the old adage that, on screen, less means more, you'll undoubtedly see it here.

The only thing that really troubled Laughton were the children. He didn't like them, and Mitchum was left to help with their performances, as Elsa Lancaster, Laughton's widow, confirms. Perhaps this is why their scenes look a little like those in another, slightly different, film. But even this works, since they are from a totally different emotional world to the adults.

The script for the film was more Laughton's than that of James Agee, whose last film this was always reckoned to be. In fact, Laughton did turn to him for help, but they could not agree and he complained loudly that Agee's version was 'as big as a telephone book'. We'll probably never know the truth of the matter.

But the fact remains that *Night of the Hunter*, though not without its faults, chiefly when it becomes a little too obviously arty, is one of those films that seems resonant from beginning to end.

As the title suggests, most of it was shot at night, and thus the hymn that forms the film's ironic refrain becomes that much more chilling: 'Leaning, leaning! Safe and secure from all alarms! Leaning, leaning! Leaning on the everlasting arms!'

FIRES WERE STARTED

Directed by Humphrey Jennings
UK, 1943, 78 minutes

Most people, if asked to name the finest British director, would probably plump for Hitchcock, Lean or Powell. Some, however, would say Humphrey Jennings, once described by Lindsay Anderson as the only true poet of the English cinema. *Fires Were Started* is his most celebrated film, and undoubtedly a classic.

Jennings was a poet and a painter too – a man, in fact, of the widest possible culture. But he saw a way of combining everything in what may seem to be the most unyielding cinematic *métier* of documentary. When he died young in 1950, he had only worked for 17 years as a film-maker, all of them in what we would now call docu-drama.

Fires Were Started is his longest work, made in 1943. But it was not the only extraordinary film he made, for the GPO Film Unit before the last world war and for the Crown Film Unit and the Ministry of Information during it. In other hands, many of these films would have been mere propaganda made to stiffen the national mood. But in his, the views of Britain were often so powerful and so moving that people would be in tears watching them.

The nature of the images available to him are perfectly expressed in a poem he wrote, in the same year as he filmed *Heart of Britain* and *Words for Battle*, two superb shorts:

I see a thousand strange sights in the streets of London,
I see the clock on Bow Church burning in daytime,
I see a one-legged man crossing the fire on crutches,
I see three negroes and a woman with white face-powder reading music at half-past three in the morning,
I see an ambulance girl with her arms full of roses,
I see the burnt drums of the Philharmonic,
I see the green leaves of Lincolnshire carried through London on the wrecked body of an aircraft.

He called his films 'camera poems', and the characters in *Fires Were Started* were the firemen and firewomen of the Auxiliary Fire Service, working in the most heavily bombed docklands area of London.

His achievement in the film has been most potently described by David Thompson, who said of him: 'His fires, which were, like Blake's, a condition of the soul, might even have burnt down English good manners'.

The film's early scenes introduce us to the eight characters we follow – fictional but played by real firemen. One 24-hour period is dramatised. In the morning, the men leave their homes and ordinary occupations – taxis, newspaper shops etc – to start their tour of duty.

A new recruit arrives and is shown the ropes. There is a full moon due, and warning comes that a heavy attack is anticipated. Night falls and the sirens begin to wail. The unit is called out to a riverside warehouse where fire threatens an ammunition ship at anchor by the wharf. The fire is fought and finally mastered, though one man is lost and others are injured. The ship finally sails with the morning tide.

The way the story is structured provides a portrait of what was then a besieged Britain that is astonishingly intimate. Jennings's firemen are not treated in the patronising way servicemen were often depicted in post-war films of the stiff-upper-lip variety.

True, the observation is affectionate and matter-of-fact in a typically British manner. But there is humour and irony too, as in the sequence which the firemen enter their recreation room in turn as Barrett, the pianist of the group, strikes up 'One Man Went to Mow' and other popular songs of the day for the benefit of each. The fire-fighting scenes and their aftermath are remarkable, shot and edited with no melo-dramatics whatsoever.

Jennings had founded the Mass Observation movement, which collected information on the British way of life much as Malinowski had docu-mented the behaviour of the South Sea islanders. He put this to good effect in *Fires Were Started* and other films, notably the equally famous *Listen to Britain* and *Diary for Timothy*.

But, though ineffably patrician, he transcended the class cliches of the time by recognising the way war can unite disparate people and by making us think about what would have been lost if the conflict had gone the other way. When you see his wartime films, you understand the proper meaning of patriotism.

MONSIEUR VERDOUX

Directed by Charles Chaplin
With Charles Chaplin, Mady Correll, Allison Roddan, Martha Raye
USA, 1947, 125 minutes

Chaplin is often referred to as the most important artist produced by the cinema. He was dubbed at one stage the funniest man alive, and the most popular and best-known human being in the world. Yet, some time before his death in 1977, it was fashionable to prefer Buster Keaton, both as a performer and director of his own work.

Some of those who did either regarded Chaplin as a chronic sentimentalist or conversely as an icon who damaged his popular reputation
by having ideas beyond his station. The sentimentalist tag was the most
usual reason why Keaton, a very great clown, was preferred to him.

There is, however, one film which more than equalled any of the
Keaton features so justifiably admired. And that was *Monsieur Verdoux*,
made in 1947, and perversely attacked at the time for being about as
unsentimental as you could get.

It was certainly provocative. Chaplin played Verdoux, a character
inspired by Landru, the real-life seducer and murderer of rich women
who operated during the First World War, when eligible men were scarce,
and was executed soon afterwards.

The real man, though charming, was clearly evil. But Chaplin, moving
him forward in time into the thirties, makes him a victim of the Great
Depression – a redundant bank clerk attempting to find any means at his
disposal to protect his crippled wife and family by bigamously courting
and marrying rich women, securing their property and then returning
home with the booty.

You could say that in breaking the taboos of that (or any) society, Verdoux was actually illustrating its hypocrisy, since at the time the film was made the impact of the millions of war casualties, which decimated a whole European generation, was still fresh in people's minds.

Perhaps the philosophy behind *Monsieur Verdoux*, Chaplin's most pessimistic and gag-free film, was simplistic. But his sarcastic and ironic gravity was astonishing for the time.

Eventually, of course, Verdoux, doubling up as Varney, Bonheur and Floray, is caught and charged, losing everything, including his wife and son. But then he becomes the accuser – a murderer taught to kill by the society which spawned him. 'Wars, conflict,' he says in prison before his execution, 'It's all business. One murder makes a villain; millions a hero. Numbers sanctify.'

The film, in which Chaplin used sound as effectively as he ever did by dint of a clever if talky screenplay, is certainly not without humour, such as the famous sequence when Verdoux, intent on another murder, falls into the water and is saved by his victim (the gloriously obstreperous Martha Raye, who has already somehow avoided the poison he has made for her).

Verdoux is nothing like the Little Tramp whom the world loved, but a dapper, elderly man sporting a little French tash, at one point carefully cutting roses in the garden as an incinerator burns the remains of his latest victim. There is only one point at which the tramp comes to mind, and that is when Verdoux walks calmly towards his execution.

Chaplin hoped that his central character would somehow express the times in which he lived – 'he is frustrated, bitter and, at the end, pessimistic. But he is never morbid.'

The European public agreed, especially in France, where half a million people saw the film – a huge number in those days. But in America, with the McCarthy witch-hunts just beginning, Monsieur Verdoux was ludicrously considered 'communistic' and flopped badly.

Even now, it is not generally considered one of Chaplin's best films. But though hardly characteristic, it leaves an indelible memory in the mind. Few remember, incidentally, that its story was taken not only from history but from an idea by Orson Welles, who might well have thought about playing Verdoux himself.

THE MARRIAGE OF MARIA BRAUN

Directed by Rainer Werner Fassbinder
With Hanna Schygulla, Ivan Desny, Klaus Löwitsch
Germany, 1978, 119 minutes

Just as it wouldn't be possible to ignore the French New Wave in any list of the 100 best films, it's also impossible to ignore the many extraordinay works of the New German Cinema that eventually succeeded it, carrying the flag of European cinema throughout the world.

No individual flag was carried further than that of Rainer Werner Fassbinder, and *The Marriage of Maria Braun*, by far that prolific director's most successful film commercially, was a landmark, like Wim Wenders's *Kings of the Road*, in German cinema.

Perhaps it was not Fassbinder's most personal film, nor his most interesting cinematically. I'm not sure it's any better than *Fear Eats the Soul*, *The Merchant of Four Seasons*, *Bolweiser* or the giant television project taken from Alfred Doblin's *Berlin Alexanderplatz*.

But since Fassbinder always wanted to make 'German Hollywood films', and invariably insisted that his greatest wish was popular success, *The Marriage of Maria Braun*, made in 1978, is a particular triumph. He was half infatuated and half repelled by Hollywood, and the film's form shows that. But it could never have been made in America, since it takes highly political account of a whole period of German history and stamps a sour opinion of the downside of that country's post-war economic miracle on almost every frame.

Everyday Fascism was one of his pet themes – the way we are influenced by the more blatant and regretable aspects of the society in which we live. His characters' crises, a critic has rightly said, are private reenactments of the patterns of power and manipulation that surround them in society at large.

The principal role was to have been taken by Romy Schneider, Germany's biggest star of the period. But in the end Fassbinder, by this time pretty far gone down the drug road, managed to call her a 'dumb cow' in public and had thus to choose Hanna Schygulla instead.

He hadn't worked with Schygulla for several years, and her career had gone rapidly downhill after being banished from Fassbinder's circle for leading a revolt about low wages during the making of *Effie Briest*. He had told her then: 'I can't stand the sight of your face anymore. You bust my balls.'

However, he clearly relented, and in the film she plays Maria, a girl who marries a private in the German army during the Second World War, only to see him almost immediately depart for the Russian front. He is soon reported missing, and she goes to live with a black American GI. When her husband suddenly returns, she kills the GI in the heat of a quarrel and he nobly takes the rap.

While he is in prison, she saves for their future together and, participating cheerfully in the increasing prosperity of the country, also has a productive affair with her boss. Unbeknown to her, the boss gives her husband money to stay away. Finally the two meet again. By now, however, they are complete strangers to one another. Her new-found and prosperous life has suffocated their dream of love.

It is a magnificent performance from Schygulla, playing a vulnerable young woman who becomes a self-confident, independent, amazingly competent survivor but, even so, comes to a bad end, largely because of the basic corruption of her world. At one point we hear Adenauer, the West German Chancellor, solemnly promising on the radio that Germany will never rearm. Later we hear him say that the country has an inalienable right to do so.

Maria Braun is a victim of the same sort of contradiction. She wants to be faithful to her husband not because she is a good little woman but because she believes in the relationship she has privately fostered for so long. But the facts of life gradually come to decree otherwise – as, says Fassbinder, they always tend to.

The film was the great Michael Ballhaus's last as Fassbinder's cameraman, and also contained one of the best screenplays, written from the director's own outline.

In it, he allows us to identify with his heroine utterly, as she ruthlessly gets everything she wants in preparation for her reunion with her husband. But he does so for a purpose, which is to shock us into the realisation that Germany's post-war prosperity was based on a whole series of false premises, which eventually infected those who believed in it. 'Why didn't I join the Bader-Meinhof gang?' he once said.

The miracle is that Fassbinder was able, riddled with coke and other substances as he was, to direct Schygulla and the film so precisely. Apparently he even instructed her how to move her fingers.

His movies are generally about the oppressor and the oppressed. But this one was not so much about Hollywood's familiar idea of the redeeming nature of love but the fact that it is often the worst oppressor of all. In his own life, as in his art, that was certainly true.

BEAUTY AND THE BEAST

Directed by Jean Cocteau and René Clement
With Jean Marais, Josette Day
France, 1946, 90 minutes

It has often been said that Jean Cocteau was the first major poet and writer to treat the cinema with total seriousness. But actually it was the cinema that made him into a major artist. 'The movie screen,' he said, 'is the true mirror reflecting the flesh and blood of my dreams'. And one of his most poetic, dream-like films was *La Belle et La Bête*.

Watching it now, you can't quite feel its audacity as you might have at the time. Faithfully, but not totally innocently, based on the fairy-tale by Madame Leprince de Beaumont, it is almost purely visual, even if a Freudian analysis is possible. And it is certainly completely different in atmosphere and style to anything that had gone before, at least in the commercial cinema.

The team who made it, and it was a team, broke a good many rules at the urging of Cocteau. Georges Auric's memorable music didn't so much underline the visuals as frequently cut across them, reaching a synthesis at vital moments. Henri Alekan's equally extraordinary cinematography, which the studio described unsympathetically as 'white cheese', is the opposite of conventionally fantastic – 'I'm pushing Alekan in precisely the opposite direction from what fools think is poetic,' Cocteau wrote.

Alekan's black-and-white photography was sharp and unfuzzy, set in a credible French country landscape containing not just the realistic home of Beauty but also the weird, enchanted domicile of the Beast. It could almost be a documentary. Which allows us to believe anything Cocteau asks of us.

The result was a film that dared to be naive, asking its audience to revert to their childhood the better to accept its magic. It is one of Cocteau's few films that it is wiser to take at face value than to explore at the level of later, perhaps more sophisticated and certainly more pretentious, works like the two famous Orphée films.

Only when the Beast is transformed into the handsome Jean Marais and the flight to happiness provides a harmonious ending do we begin to doubt anything – apart, perhaps, from the Beast's curiously squeaky voice. But even then we are willing to suspend our disbelief. After all, isn't everything else perfectly normal?

I'm prepared to receive the argument that *Beauty and the Beast* is not Cocteau's most 'important' film, and that it does have some creaky moments. But it is probably still his most perfect, because it speaks to

so wide an audience with its intensity of vision and the emotions it inspires in us.

Watch Beauty looking into a mirror and seeing her face replaced by that of the Beast, her almost trance-like walk through the Beast's melancholy hallways, or her pacing backwards and forwards as she impatiently awaits his nightly visit (as a statue behind her follows her with its head), and you see a precisely imagined fantasy.

It's all the better for not relying on astonishing special effects but on the private thoughts of the watcher. Would that some Hollywood films today did us that honour.

The importance of Cocteau's work on film is that it embodies a number of different traditions and disciplines, and is as beholden to classical drama as it is to the avant-garde. That is why it remains so fascinating and so strong in peoples' memories.

He was almost sixty when he made *Beauty and the Beast*, his first full-length feature. But the astonishing fact is that this elderly poet had, and still has, a huge influence on the avant-garde of American film. Paradoxically, in worshipping the new in Cocteau, some of them had little idea of the traditions from which his art sprang.

RIO BRAVO

Directed by Howard Hawks
With John Wayne, Dean Martin, Angie Dickinson
USA, 1959, 141 minutes

If I had my way, there would be half a dozen westerns tucked away inside my 100 favourite movies, since it's my contention that almost everything the American cinema has to say has been said within this genre. And if I allowed my heart to rule my head, there would be half a dozen Howard Hawks movies in there too.

Westerns seem to me to express best the myths of American history and the often noble, sometimes absurd, fantasies Americans have about themselves. As for Hawks, he was a master of the genre but also a master of most others too – an intuitive director whose extraordinary subtleties could make even a piece of pure entertainent like *Bringing Up Baby* into a blazing classic.

Combine my love of westerns and my admiration for Hawks and you have *Rio Bravo*, a great film and one of the most acutely personal he ever made. I have to tell you, with some shame, that when the film arrived in Britain in 1959, the *Guardian's* review (not mine) read as follows: 'Rio Bravo is a typical Western of this age of the long-winded, large screen. It lasts for 140 minutes and it contains enough inventiveness to make do for about half that time. It is, in fact, a soporific blockbuster. John Wayne leads its cast.'

Thus we disposed of a piece of flawless story-telling, totally admirable in its basic simplicity and outward lack of guile, and of a great and pretty selfless performance from Wayne, who helped Dean Martin give by far the best portrait of his career.

Hawks always said that he made *Rio Bravo* as a riposte to *High Noon*, in which Gary Cooper's town sheriff went 'running around the town like a chicken with his head off asking for help'. That wasn't his idea of a good western hero. To him, it was both politically incorrect and morally reprehensible.

Sheriff Wayne in *Rio Bravo* needs as much help as Cooper when he imprisons a murderer and gunmen lay siege to the jail. But he gets it by being his flawed, sometimes comic, but fundamentally decent and honourable self. It even makes the drunken deputy (Martin) stand up and fight, and it also teaches the sheriff himself to temper his determined insistence on independence at all costs simply by forming the oddest of partnerships. Beside the sheriff and the drunk are Ricky Nelson's silly young gun, Angie Dickinson's lady gambler, with whom Wayne constantly spars, and Walter Brennan's toothless veteran.

In all this, it is a deeply traditional western. The way it is worked out, however, is anything but that. It's a long film with a pretty slim plot and lots of comic diversions, like Wayne modelling a pair of bloomers for Dickinson, who tells him: 'Those things have possibilities, sheriff. But not on you.'

So firmly is the whole thing based on character, however, that you come out of it feeling you've seen something special about humanity in general. It's a feelgood movie that for once rings true, even as you admit a certain strand of orthodoxy, even cliche, seen in westerns over and over again. It's also pretty exciting because, though you know things will probably turn out okay, Hawks never lets you be quite sure of it. Someone's going to have to die.

Watching the film, you won't see any great vistas like Ford's *Monument Valley* or backdrops like Budd Boetticher's *Lonesome Pine* nestling in the Alabama Hills. This is just a scrubby little township with a seedy-looking hotel, a saloon, a jail and nothing whatsoever to commend it bar the characters who live there.

If Ford had made the picture, it wouldn't have been possible to avoid a larger cast and more of an idea of the community at large. If Anthony Mann, another great maker of westerns, had done so, there would have been more directorial philosophising and the psychology would have been less basic.

What we get from Hawks is austerity, rigour and intensity. The result certainly seems more real than any fake attempts at sophistication might have been.

Of course, there are a dozen different ways to make westerns, and Hawks's way in *Rio Bravo* lacks the epic nature of *Red River*, the greater flamboyance (and Mitchum) of *El Dorado*, and the sheer if nonsensical fun of *Hatari!* But it's a better film than any of them because of its concentration and the deep feelings that Hawks clearly poured into it.

They say he modelled the Wayne character on himself, but if so it was surely unconsciously. What he did do was allow a great script by Jules Furthman and Leigh Brackett to flow as naturally as possible, while burnishing it with bits and pieces of extemporising, right down to what the actors wore, like Martin's soiled sweatshirt and dirty old hat.

When he showed Jack Warner the film, he said: 'We hired Dean Martin. When's he going to be in this picture?' Hawks replied: 'He's the funny-looking guy in the old hat'. 'Holy smoke,' said Warner. 'Is that Dean Martin?' It was, and in a way it was his picture.

BRIEF ENCOUNTER

Directed by David Lean
With Celia Johnson, Trevor Howard
UK, 1945, 100 minutes

> Alec: You know what's happened, don't you?
> Laura: Yes – yes, I do.
> Alec: I've fallen in love with you.
> Laura: Yes – I know.
> Alec: Tell me honestly, my dear, please tell me honestly if what I believe is true...
> Laura: What do you believe?
> Alec: That it's the same with you – that you've fallen in love too.
> Laura: It sounds so silly.
> Alec: Why?
> Laura: I know you so little.
> Alec: It's true though – isn't it?
> Laura: Yes – it's true.

Tear-jerkers are part and parcel of the cinema, however much we refuse to accord them status as we bring out our hankies. But when David Lean's *Brief Encounter* was previewed in Rochester, a coarse laugh from near the front enlivened the first love scene. And by the end of the film, the whole audience was rolling in the aisles.

The cinema was right next to Chatham dockyards, which might explain the furore about this very middle-class tragic romance. Later, the critics took so different a view that Rank advertised it in the industrial north as being good 'in spite of the wild praise of the London critics'.

Many years later, I did an interview with Lean who told me that the French encomiums about the film's innate understanding of the English middle classes, underlining the fact that the lovers never go to bed with each other, are spurious. 'They might well have screwed like rabbits in real life,' he said, 'But this was real life as J. Arthur Rank insisted on us seeing it'.

Even so, the reticence made for a classic film, very much more than a theatrical adaptation, with Celia Johnson as the married woman and Trevor Howard as the doctor who falls for her giving superb and brilliantly judged performances.

No matter how often the film is mocked and parodied, most notably by Mike Nichols and Elaine May, or sneered at by such as Pauline Kael ('There is not a breath of air in it'), it remains extraordinarily moving. Only the comic relief provided by the attendant working classes ('Come off it, mother, be a pal!' 'I'll give you mother, you saucy upstart!') seems false now.

Even at the time, it defied most of the rules of the box office, having no star names, an unhappy ending, unglamorous locations, and lovers approaching middle age. It was a risk that came off triumphantly, which is why it remains a piece of cinema almost everybody who sees it remembers with perhaps nostalgic but genuine enough affection.

Of course Lean made many more spectacular films – *Great Expectations*, which was his next project, is undoubtedly the greatest Dickens adaptation for the screen, and shows a master editor as well as a magnificent film-maker at work. But the simplicity of *Brief Encounter* – always one of the most difficult things to achieve – is unsurpassed, like it or not.

Lean put nothing in front of the main thrust of the story, which shows a happily married woman with a nice husband and children meeting and falling for a man with whom there can be no future, since guilt will always get in the way.

Curiously, Johnson, whose performance anchors the story, loathed making films, and was terrified at the thought of holding this one together with a then inexperienced Trevor Howard at her side. Though in the end Howard gives us a superb portrait, he couldn't understand the scene in which Laura, having been begged by Alec to come to the flat he's borrowed from a friend, eventually arrives there, whereupon the two start to talk about the weather and the damp wood on the fire.

As Kevin Brownlow tells it in his book about Lean, Howard said: 'David, will you please explain this to me. This is a fucking awful scene.' To which Lean replied: 'What's fucking awful about it?' 'Well,' said Howard, 'They know jolly well this chap's borrowed a flat, they know exactly why she's coming back to him, why doesn't he fuck her? All this talk about the wood being damp and that sort of stuff…' 'Look, Trevor,' said Lean, 'Have you ever been out with a girl… and you know that you're going to make love, whether it's her place or your place… And then when you get there and the door is shut and you're alone, everything's changed and there's a kind of embarrassment that you hadn't got when you were surrounded by people?' 'Oh God, you are a funny chap.' 'Funny chap or not, that's the way we're doing the scene, now come on.'

Whatever might or might not have happened, the scene in the flat is, of course, interrupted by the arrival of Valentine Dyall as the owner. Dyall was later to be famous as the lugubrious Man in Black. But at no point in his career did he do a more unfortunate thing than disturbing those lovers and their damp wood.

WR: MYSTERIES OF THE ORGANISM

Directed by Dusan Makavejev
With Milena Dravic, Jagoda Kaloper, Jackie Curtis as herself
Yugoslavia, 1971, 120 minutes

When Dusan Makavejev's *WR: Mysteries of the Organism* was presented at the Academy Cinema in Oxford Street, at that time the premier art house in London, it was only after some tribulations with the Censor, who objected to the brief views of an erect penis, albeit one encased in plaster. Eventually, the Academy was allowed to get away with it, after saying that it wouldn't screen the film at all unless it was complete.

Later, the situation was compounded by the fact that a great many people referred mistakenly to the film as '*WR: Mysteries of the Orgasm*'. Makavejev's film, however, controversial as it was in the early seventies, is not a sex film. But it certainly is a film about sex, since WR stands for Wilhelm Reich, a close associate of Freud and a Marxist who believed, among other things, that sexual freedom was the true expression of communism.

This was the highly original Yugoslavian director's fourth film, and was easily his most audacious – a landmark in the film-making of the time, after which Makavejev never had quite the same success.

The first Makavejev film I ever saw was *Innocence Unprotected*, the marvellously stitched together story of Dragoljub Aleksic, a Yugoslavian strongman who made the first Serbian talkie in 1942 and got into trouble with the occupying Germans when it became an outrageous success.

The film quotes liberally from the 1942 dream fantasy, interviews some of its veteran actors, and then cuts in and out of newsreel footage of what was actually going on in Yugoslavia at the time. The result is a remarkably funny, moving and nostalgic collage based upon the methods used in *WR*.

WR begins like a documentary, shot in America, where Reich had died in prison after succeeding in being expelled from both Communist Russia and Nazi Germany. Friends and disciples, and even his barber, are interviewed before we move to a girl called Milena in Yugoslavia who, riotously, tries to prove Reich's theories in the context of being a Communist Party member.

Of course this is a political and moral satire and a lot else besides, again manipulating various films and newsreels in and out of the proceedings. One of the films is Chiaureli's *The Vow*, a 1947 Soviet hagiography of Stalin of unbelievable banality, and another is an early thirties and tinted German Sexpol movie showing love-making in a meadow.

Added to that there is a sequence with Jackie Curtis, the famous Warholian transvestite, with the editor of *Screw* magazine having the above-mentioned penis moulded in plaster, and another with a woman painter who did a series of pictures of men and women masturbating (Reichian tension-releasing).

All this and much more is put together with what one can only call magisterial abandon, so that it not only makes sense but also makes hay with our usual preconceptions. Makavejev always used to say that he wanted to put two and two together and make five – the original purpose of Eisenstein's theory of dialectical montage. Unfortunately, he added cheekily, Eisenstein didn't have the humour to do it properly.

Makavejev certainly did, and created a unique film in so doing, especially within a Yugoslavia still balancing precariously between East and West at the time. Alas, after *WR* came *Sweet Movie*, a grave disappointment, and Makavejev's transformation into a peripatetic international director who could never quite hit the same mark again.

But since he's an old friend of mine, and one of the most stimulating of companions, I always hope he will. And for four of his earlier films alone – *Man Is Not A Bird, The Switchboard Operator, Innocence Unprotected,* and *WR* – he deserves all the fame and fortune that has been latterly denied him.

THE MUSIC ROOM

Directed by Satyajit Ray
With Chabi Biswas
India, 1960, 120 minutes

Once, after I had dinner with Satyajit Ray, the great Bengali director, at his Calcutta home, he presented me with his book, *My Films, Their Films.* Inscribed on the fly page was: 'To Derek Malcolm, who sometimes likes my films'.

Considering the fact that I think there are five or six of them worthy of consideration as one of the best films of all time, I felt the remark, though humourous in intent, was a tiny bit undeserved.

One of those films, of course, is *Pather Panchali,* the very first film he made in 1956 and the initial part of the extraordinary 'Apu' trilogy. Another is *Charaluta,* a study of middle-class relationships and disappointed love, that is as unique and memorable as the tribulations of the peasant Apu.

But the film I would select above both is *Jalsaghar,* or *The Music Room,* which proves beyond doubt that this multi-talented writer, composer, illustrator and film-maker, who was sometimes accused of being more Western than Indian, was no such thing. Though influenced by Jean Renoir, whom he aided with his Indian film *The River,* and bowled over as a young man with De Sica's *Bicycle Thieves,* Ray's chief debt remained to Rabindranath Tagore, the Indian poet, writer and philosopher with whom he studied as a teenager.

True, his films were deeply alien to those of the commercial Indian cinema of his time – as subtle and delicate as they were melodramatic and obvious. But though he 'saw all the film classics I could cram in' when he was sent to London as a young man by the advertising agency with which he worked, *The Music Room* proves beyond doubt that he was as Indian as any other national director, and merely more capable of being appreciated by the whole world.

The film is an elaboration by Ray of a short story by Tara Shanker Bannerjee, and the protagonist is an elderly *zamindar* (the equivalent of our landed gentry) who, in the late twenties, tries to stop the advent of progress which he thinks is destroying the culture he knows and loves.

His wilful refusal to face uncomfortable facts leads him to organise one last party in his dilapidated music room, despite the fact that he has to sell his jewellery to do so. Despite that, he forges ahead, raising his glass to the portraits of his ancestors as a spider picks its way over a painting of his own florid youth. Bats fly down the corridor, and in a vast and now-tarnished mirror he confronts himself.

The party is somehow organised, the most expensive dancer of the day hired, and Ganguli, the rich upstart it is designed to put down, invited. Finally, as the dancer finishes, and Ganguli makes to throw her an extravagant rupee tribute, his wrist is held by the crook of the old man's once-elegant Bond Street walking stick. It is the host who will pay, and even more generously.

The film has many such marvellous moments – the old man's ancient ceremonial elephant is contrasted with the horn of Ganguli's car, blaring out 'Colonel Bogey' as it passes. This is one of Ray's most magnificently visual films, thanks to the superb camerawork of Subrata Mitra. But it is also about music too, with Ray's equally ravishing score showing us that the old aristocrat's appreciation of high art was not simply an attempt to show off.

Ray was criticised at the time for falling in love with his central character and the glorious past he represents. But that is to take no account of the fact that the *zamindar* is an absurd and pathetic creature whose life has lost its meaning after the death of his wife and son, and of his whole class too.

Yet the great performance of Chabi Biswas in the part also demands our affection, and we can share in his regret for the past even as we mock him. Ray insists he is neither hero nor anti-hero – just a lonely old man whose nostalgia leads him into absurdity but still one last triumph of a sort.

Ray was constantly criticised in some Indian circles for not being Indian enough, not being radical enough in either content or style, and adhering to an old-fashioned liberal humanism that would put him in the good books of the West.

In the end, however, he became a monument to Indian cinema like no other, with several trunks full of awards under his bed, which he sometimes showed visitors as if to prove first that he'd got them and second that he wasn't vulgar enough to display them. What you can certainly say about him is that, like all great film-makers, he belonged to the world as much as to his own nation.

The Music Room, however, leaves no doubt at all where his heart lay. It was with his own people, warts and all.

THE KILLING OF A CHINESE BOOKIE

Directed by John Cassavetes
With Ben Gazzara, Timothy Carey, Seymour Cassel, Azizi Johari
USA, 1976, 109 minutes

John Cassavetes, the actor, writer and director, was unquestionably one of the most influential American film-makers of the post-war era – a big claim since he only had one hit movie and made many which were only shown in art houses. But at one time there was scarcely a film-maker, in or out of Hollywood, who wasn't emboldened by his improvisatory work and his extraordinary capacity to achieve exceptional performances from his casts. He has been called the first American independent, and he was certainly one of the most notable.

His hit film was *A Woman Under the Influence*, in which Gena Rowlands, his wife, was celebrated for her portrait of a family woman pitched into manic psychosis by the pressures upon her. Otherwise, Cassavetes was always more praised than seen and some of the fulsome tributes to him when he died in 1989 were nauseatingly hypocritical.

Cassavetes acted so that he could make his own films in the way he wanted. *Shadows*, his first film, made well away from Hollywood in 1959, was a huge *succes d'estime*, which prompted Hollywood to sign him up for *Too Late Blues* and *A Child Is Waiting*. But both films were compromised and flopped, and he decided to pursue his own way with funds gathered from parts like *The Dirty Dozen* and *Rosemary's Baby*.

The result was a posse of films, usually inhabited by Rowlands, Ben Gazzara, Peter Falk and Seymour Cassel, actors who never did anything better away from his baton, which were called indulgent and disorganised by those who hated them, and adored by his supporters for their passionately truthful depiction of American life.

One of them was *The Killing of a Chinese Bookie* – a film which displays most of the faults of his kind of on-the-hoof film-making, and all the virtues. He always used to say that the emotion in his films was improvised but the lines written. There's no doubt, though, that when he let his actors loose on the set there were considerable surprises in store.

Ben Gazzara is the star of *Killing* – the story of the owner of the Crazy Horse West, a failing LA strip joint he is determined to keep open because it's the only thing he's built up from scratch in his somewhat tawdry life. In order to remain solvent, he has to kill a Chinese bookie for the Mob, and the sequence in which he breaks into the old man's luxurious apartment and does the job is as terrifying as anything in *The Godfather*, performed virtually in silence late at night.

But the film is as much a treatise on the sleazier side of showbiz, and on persistent hope in almost ludicrously unhopeful circumstances, as it is a thriller. It's about a man hanging on for dear life to dear life. As such, you could call it pretentious, bombastic, indulgent and full of actorly tropes, concocted by Cassavetes and Gazzara as they progress through a waywardly philosophical tale. Why, then, can one simply not forget it?

It's principally because of its accurate summation of one man's American dream in all its absurdity – the girls in the strip joint are nurtured almost as part of him, and the club itself, which looks like a particularly seedy purgatory to us, is clearly heaven to him. You can see why he will do anything to save it, and feel the sincerity of even the most portentous of his monologues.

Above all, Cassavetes orchestrates the whole thing almost as if it is a dream from which we are about to wake up. But even his most eccentric worlds have a point in them which seems to parallel our own more mundane lives. Most of Cassavetes's films are like that. They don't make you fantasise, like the best of Hollywood. They face the messiness of life awkwardly and then turn to you and say: 'But it's the truth, isn't it?'

LA COLLECTIONNEUSE

Directed by Eric Rohmer
With Patrick Bauchau, Haydee Politoff, Daniel Pommereulle
France, 1967, 100 minutes

Most people admire the sheer obstinacy of Eric Rohmer, who continues to make rather donnishly talky films, generally grouped together under a vague theme, long after his sort of very French and certainly intellectual cinema went out of vogue.

Not everybody actually likes them. They are sometimes thought just too damned civilised. But a good many older critics, and certainly older cinema-goers, still find them a benison amongst the crude clatter of Hollywood and the often boringly predictable 'art' of many of Rohmer's European contemporaries.

'The Six Moral Tales' is probably his most famous series – he's just finished 'The Four Seasons' – and most would vote for *My Night With Maud* or *Claire's Knee* as the best of them. Each is a variation on the theme of a man committed to a woman but deflected by a chance meeting with another. My favourite, however, is *La Collectionneuse*, which is eccentric

since it was something like a dry run for the aforementioned international hits.

But it seems to me that its freshness makes up for its lack of a more sophisticated perfection of form. And talking of perfect forms, which one is not supposed to do today, Haydee Politoff's bikini-clad young collector of men, who is the fulcrum of the drama, adds an erotic frisson even *Claire's Knee* didn't quite manage.

Rohmer's camera fixes on her as she walks, bronzed and half naked along the beach, as if to see if he can analyse not just her body but the nature which leads her to sleep with a different partner each night, virtually without thought or more than momentary pleasure.

The real central character, however, is Adrien, the good-looking but decidedly solemn intellectual who decides that he will not be seduced, much as he would like to be, but instead will wait for the English representative of true love, briefly seen at the start of the film.

He shares a St Tropez villa with the temptress, and a rather more immediately likeable painter (Daniel Pommereulle, a real-life artist) who has a less pure sexual orientation.

Rohmer analyses his three leading characters rather as if they were moths flying a little too near the light of desire. It's nothing like a conventionally romantic or erotic film, but its hazy aura of summer in the South of France gives it at least an air of romantic and/or sexual expectation.

What Rohmer is on about, of course, is the way human nature plays the game of love, with hesitation, subterfuge and often perversity. He has constantly returned to that theme ever since, with films as full of dialogue as most nowadays eschew it. The moral dilemmas are interior, but the film-making is precise and objective. There is irony to spare, but little overt comedy and no parody.

Rohmer has said that his films reach out only to the small minority prepared for the cinema's less spectacular pleasures, and he certainly adhered to the tenets of the critic and writer André Bazin more than his fellow critics and film-makers within the influential Cahiers group (who in the end rejected him as reactionary).

Whether he actually is sometimes tiresomely old-fashioned is a moot point. Certainly he has more in common with Renoir, the old master of French cinema, than either Godard, Truffaut, Rivette or Chabrol, though like them he recognises a debt to Hollywood's masters.

His point, well made in *La Collectionneuse* as in all the 'Moral Tales', is that the secret dilemmas of individuals are as important as the those of 'the people' or the state. But if that seems obvious, the films themselves seldom are. They are variations on a theme that almost seems to have a musical dimension – fluent, sometimes surprising and always intriguing to listen to, if seldom powerful enough to rip your emotions apart.

Drama, for Rohmer, is made up of a number of frequently small incidents which culminate in an inevitable denouement. There are many kinds of film-making, but Rohmer's would be very difficult to beat within the confines of his chosen *métier*.

THE PHILADELPHIA STORY

Directed by George Cukor
With Cary Grant, Katherine Hepburn, James Stewart
USA, 1940, 112 minutes

George Cukor has often been called a pre-eminent director of women. And that he was, like certain other gay film-makers. Katherine Hepburn, Greta Garbo, Ingrid Bergman, Judy Garland and Constance Bennett could testify to that. It would be more accurate, however, to cast him as a film-maker who paid particular attention to performance in general, and relationships in particular.

But his true significance is that he was one of the few who survived Hollywood's often cavalier treatment of original talent, despite the blow of being fired by David Selznick a few days into the shooting of *Gone with the Wind*, after coaching Vivien Leigh, a surprise choice for the central part. Cukor had just about the longest continuous career of any major director who worked within the mainstream.

Whether such a sensibility could exist now is a moot point, since when you look at the sort of movies he might have been asked to direct now, were he still at work, you long for the wit, humanity and, above all, the sense of style evinced by such classics as *The Philadelphia Story*.

The film is not, perhaps, the funniest romantic comedy ever made, since Cukor attempted to pitch Donald Ogden Stewart and Waldo Salt's adaptation of the Phillip Barry play into the realms of ironic social significance by suggesting that it isn't only the rich who have vices and the poor virtues. But considering the talkative nature of the film, it moves marvellously and contains performances it would be very hard to beat because they are based on the wit of character rather than lines.

Besides, it isn't all talk. The opening sequence, in fact, contains no words at all. Cary Grant, as Hepburn's former husband, is thrown out of the front door of her wealthy parents' ritzy home in Philadelphia. When Hepburn, soon to be married again to a less dissolute lover, appears, she breaks one of his favourite golf clubs, throws them after him and slams the door. Grant doesn't give up, and rings the doorbell again. When Hepburn answers, he pushes her in the face.

This silent sequence is perfectly timed and tells us everything. Admittedly we are in a sense primed, since the two stars had appeared before as antagonists, notably in Cukor's own *Sylvia Scarlett* and in Howard Hawks's *Bringing Up Baby*. And Hepburn's furious reaction turned to advantage the previous reputation she had acquired as arrogant and mannish, and thus box-office poison.

Actually, it was she who got the play, in which she starred on Broadway, made into a film, since she acquired the movie rights and sold them to MGM with the proviso that she was the star and had the choice of director and co-stars. It seems extraordinary now that she had left Hollywood in high dudgeon before this film, feeling totally unappreciated by the public. But this was the thirties, when women stars were liked for their vulnerability rather than their independence.

The point is that Cukor's skill at using her negative image and turning it round so successfully – the film was a huge hit – was typical of the man. He knew exactly what he was doing and, like Hawks, was able to make the very best of good material.

Cukor has often been attacked for his general obedience to the studio system, his insistence on not interfering with the given values of a screenplay, and the commercial appeal of most of his films. At his weakest he could indeed be pedestrian (witness *My Fair Lady*). But at his best he showed how good the studio system could be. He had taste, style and humanity. And his films look better now than they ever did because of it.

MANILA: IN THE CLAWS OF DARKNESS

Directed by Lino Brocka
With Rafael Roco Jr, Hilda Coronel
Philippines, 1975, 125 minutes

When Lino Brocka died in a car crash, the Philippines lost its outstanding director – a man who, despite the constraints of an almost totally commercial Tagalog industry and vicious censorship under the dictator Marcos, succeeded in making half a dozen films of great power and universal appeal.

Often they were produced cheaply and virtually on the run, with Marcos's men instructed to prevent a rebel like Brocka telling the truth about the dictatorship and the poverty it did not create but did little or nothing to alleviate. In the end, however, Brocka's international reputation saved him.

It was shored up when *Jaguar*, about a guard who looks after a middle-class apartment block and keeps his nose out of trouble but eventually gets dragged down into endemic corruption and criminality, became the first film from his country to be shown in competition at Cannes. He remained an implacable opponent of the regime to the end, and his early death made him into an instant legend.

Manila: In the Claws of Darkness is the most impressive of his film noir, made with bows to the American cinema, to Italian neo-realism and to his own country's long tradition of star-driven melodramas or 'bomba' sex movies, but with the force of a Third-World director determined to say something relevant about his own society.

It's the richly romantic but realistic odyssey of a boy named Julio, who arrives from the country to Manila to search for his lost childhood sweetheart. The darkness of the title refers to the capital itself which, said Brocka, exerts an invisible force on the lives of its people.

Brocka exposes the exploitation of the city's construction workers, some of whom were killed or injured when Marcos jerry-built a huge new complex to house his annual Film Festival, to which Mrs Marcos invited no less a figure than Satyajit Ray as President of the Jury. The film also looks at the almost sub-human existence of Manila's slum dwellers, whose children pick through huge rubbish dumps for something to sell.

Finally, it casts its eye over the noctural underground of the city, where male and female prostitutes ply their trade. Brocka was gay himself, and half-fascinated and half-repelled by the scene which meets the innocent boy as he scours the brothels of the city, only to find his girl has been enslaved by the elderly Chinese whorehouse owner who has made her his common-law wife.

In this situation there can be no such thing as a happy ending. The boy murders the brothel owner and dies as yet another victim of the big city.

The film has several outstanding sequences, such as when the boy first discovers the fate of his sweetheart, and when he finally decides to take the law into his own hands, confirming the Tagalog saying that when a human being is in a desperate situation a sharp knife is the only means of survival. But Brocka's painting of life in the corrupt, teeming and polluted city of Manila is the movie's chief glory.

It's an unforgettable portrait which also invites interpretation as an allegory for the whole of the underdeveloped world. The girl's name means happiness and paradise, the boy's means patience, Ah Tek, the brothel owner, represents money (*atik*) and the recruiter of young girls for him is Mrs Cruz, a reference to the cross they have to bear. But though deeply romantic, the film never lets go of its central thrust – that no one has a chance in this society unless protected by the authorities or able to pay the price.

Brocka made nearly 50 films, some of which were unashamedly commercial. One of them, *Bayan Ko* (*My Country*) had to be smuggled into France for showing at Cannes, where Brocka announced that it had been banned in his home country. But even Marcos could not stop him, and he and a few others made the seventies and early eighties a golden age for Tagalog films in a country in which the population are still among the most avid film-goers in the world.

PAKEEZAH

Directed by Kamal Amrohi
With Ashok Kumar, Meena Kumari
1971, India, 175 minutes

The notion that the Indian commercial cinema, which still churns out more films per year than Hollywood, is total dross, made for the illiterate masses and seen by no one even slightly sophisticated, dies hard. But it was always nonsense and, even today, when it could be claimed that India's cinema has been technically strengthened but culturally badly weakened by Western influences, it's not at all true.

It certainly wasn't in the post-war decades that produced a whole series of film-makers, stars, musicians and playback singers worthy of anyone's attention. I have sound-tracks from the forties, fifties and sixties that

combine Indian classical, folk and traditional music with memorable skill. Would they were videos of the films themselves.

Among these directors was the Muslim Kamal Amrohi, whose *Pakeezah* (*Pure Heart*) qualifies as one of the most extraordinary musical melodramas ever made – 'poetry, fantasy and nostalgia rolled into one on an epic scale', as one Indian critic has said. Amrohi was a writer and poet in Urdu and Hindi as well as director, though he only made four films. *Pakeezah* was his third, and had been planned years before it could be made as a starring vehicle for Amrohi himself and his third wife Meena Kumari, the famous Hindi tragedienne.

Production was finally started in 1964, but when the two separated it was postponed indefinitely half-way through. Fortunately, Amrohi finally persuaded a by then somewhat raddled and alcoholic but still beautiful Kumari to complete it in the early seventies. But the story of its making, dramatic as it was, paled in comparison with the delirious telling of the story itself.

Set in Muslim Lucknow at the turn of the century, its central character, as so often in Indian films which go back in time, is a courtesan and dancer who dreams of leaving her life behind, but gets rejected by her lover's family as unmarriageable and dies giving birth in a graveyard.

The daughter (also played by Kumari) grows up in her mother's profession, admired and desired by men for everything but a respectable marriage, and is even prevented from seeing her father. She then falls for a mysterious stranger who turns out to be her father's nephew. When the marriage is forbidden, she is forced to dance at her lover's arranged wedding.

There, her father at last recognises her and claims her as his child, and she's able to marry and leave her past behind. The feel-good ending doesn't quite undermine what has gone before, which is a wonderful if sometimes unwitting lesson in the hypocrisy of the time towards women.

If there is nothing special about the plot, the way it is accomplished is often astounding. Amrohi, who also wrote the script and even some of the lyrics, saturates the screen not only with some amazing colour photography but a swirling romanticism that somehow never tips over into the laughable, even when Kumari, asked her name by a priest, rushes guiltily away when a servant answers Pakeezah ('pure'). Indeed this is one of the most notable sequences of the film.

Added to that, the musical score from Ghulam Mohammed and Naushad was supremely touching, providing singer Lata Mangeshkar with at least two songs everyone in India still knows today ('Chalte, Chalte' and 'Inhe Logone Ne').

The film certainly reminds one of the Ezra Pound observation that sex 'insofar as it is not a purely physiological mechanism, lies in the domain of aesthetics'. And those Indian directors who persistently offer their epics to the West minus the songs do not do themselves a favour. It's primarily in this area that the uncensored inner meanings of their films reside.

Pakeezah, often shown in its shorter but not better version of 125 minutes, is a case in point. Each song illustrates either the implicit tragedy of the story or the hopes of those in it, bound by tradition but striving for a fairer world.

Other Indian popular films may be subtler, like Guru Dutt's *Pyaasa*, also the story of a prostitute. Few, however, have quite the force and romantic conviction of Amrohi's. He never struck gold again, and nor did Kumari, whose last film this was. But gold *Pakeezah* definitely is.

FAT CITY

Directed by John Huston
With Stacy Keach, Jeff Bridges, Susan Tyrrell
USA, 1972, 100 minutes

Though it is extremely difficult to make much sense of John Huston's work taken as a whole, there's not much doubt that he made some outstanding films as well as some that were pretty awful. Among the best were *The Maltese Falcon, The Treasure of the Sierre Madre, The Asphalt Jungle, The African Queen, Heaven Knows, Mr Allison, The Red Badge of Courage, Wise Blood* and *The Dead* – a formidable list. But the best of all, though by no means the most popular because of its downbeat subject matter, was *Fat City*.

One thing one can always rely on in Huston films is the excellent use of either intelligent actors or personable stars. Humphrey Bogart, Robert Mitchum, Deborah Kerr and Katherine Hepburn, to say nothing of his own father, Walter Huston, were never better than under his direction. Nor was Stacy Keach, as the broken-down boxer at the centre of *Fat City*.

What fascinated Huston, once an amateur boxer, were the bottom rungs, almost the lower depths, of a dangerous profession – the losers, who are indeed often more interesting than the winners. Keach is Billy Tully, a twenty-nine-year-old who was once a contender but lost the biggest fight of his career and then his wife before relapsing into alcoholism. Even so he contemplates a come-back. When he meets a promising young nineteen-year-old (Jeff Bridges), he encourages him to sign up with his old manager and begins to live through him. But the downward spiral continues.

The setting – the tenements and bars inhabited by those who have failed but still cling to their illusions of success – is beautifully done. Working with the material provided for him by Leonard Gardner from his own novel, Huston's theme is clearly the loneliness of the long-distance survivor. He's a man who can't have effective relationships, or get his life sorted out. He lives in a fantasy world full of might-have-beens. He can't admit his hopelessness, even to himself.

Kris Kristofferson's 'Help Me Make it Through The Night' is used as a musical counterpoint to the drama, which ends on a note of hope when the boxer gets himself together enough to return to the ring and win. Even then, however, Huston undercuts the triumph by showing us not just that our 'hero' has so exhausted himself that he has to be told he's won, but by concentrating too on the loser, who may well become another Billy Tully. Besides, it is only one fight, a first and probably last step on the doubtful road to full recovery.

Keach's performance is matched by Susan Tyrrell's as the woman who has taken up with him and is also an alcoholic. But as much as anything it is the accuracy of this microcosm of the world that is so impressive, and Huston's innate sympathy with his motley characters. For once he's not trying to gild the lily with picturesque effects, nor exhibiting his capacity to charm or entertain an audience into submission. Here there is a real emotional commitment to his subject matter.

Most of his work, however, couldn't be categorised as coming from a director of real personality, even though he played larger-than-life outside his work. His best films are generally the result of a good story, a fine script and acting from well-chosen casts. This is not to denigrate him but to suggest that there are some film-makers whose efforts depend more on their material than others, and who can't invent something out of nothing through sheer skill.

Given the right material – and it was as often as not bleak and pessimistic – Huston was capable of the kind of work you can't quite get out of your head.

KES

Directed by Ken Loach
With David Bradley, Colin Welland
UK, 1969, 112 minutes

Ken Loach, the most modest of directors, would probably say he had a lot to be modest about – that his team should be equally praised. And it is certainly true that you don't look for visually imaginative work from him, though a writer in *Sight and Sound* who suggested not long ago that he couldn't even frame a shot properly was talking through the wrong hole. In fact, Loach has always said that if you notice the camerawork there's something wrong with the story.

What he struggles to find is the truth of any given situation through good casting, scripts which often seem improvised but are not, and the courage of his strong and unwavering left-leaning political convictions. At his best, Loach is a director able to make the particular into the universal, and to appeal to audiences the world over. The early *Kes* is such a film and, at the last reckoning, so were *Riff-Raff* and *Raining Stones*.

Kes is undoubtedly one of the most remarkable films about education, or the lack of it, ever made. Its main theme was perhaps a little obvious – if you give even a so-called dunce some kind of chance, the result can surprise even himself and certainly his teachers. Essentially it's a schematic film, but who cares when its incidentals are as good as its main thrust, which is never sentimentalised and maintains the right to be angry as well as touching and funny.

Kes is the kestrel found and trained by a young Barnsley boy from a broken home (marvellously played by David Bradley). He virtually refuses education at the local school, which, though inadequate, is never shown as wholly awful. Encouraged by a sympathetic teacher, he finds some sort of hope in his new interest, even though his kind of social deprivation is always likely to stamp it out.

What adds immeasurably to the film's sympathy and power are the incidental scenes of school life in the northern town of Barnsley. There are two I'll never forget. One has a tiny boy lining up outside the head's study, probably for a beating, and crying his excuses for recalcitrance to authority. The tenderness displayed here mixes with the hilarity in a way very few directors could even begin to achieve.

The other has the ex-wrestler Brian Glover as the sports master taking his boys out onto the field and, to the strains of the BBC's old *Sportsnight* signature tune, acting out a football fantasy that has him behaving more like a child than his charges. This is a classic sequence that says everything about the English and their propensity never quite to grow up.

It's this sort of thing that proclaims Loach a nearly great and certainly greatly cherishable director, since it it so much more than merely leavening his political points with humour. Who, for instance, can possibly forget Ricky Tomlinson's naked building worker in *Riff-Raff* climbing from his bath in a new building to face a posse of surprised clients brought in by one of the suits?

This is not to downgrade the serious, some say over-earnest, side of Loach's work, which invariably deals with the injustice of uncaring capitalism and invokes a properly socialist alternative. It's just to emphasise what a very good film-maker he is when encouraged by a good writer like Barry Hines (*Kes*) or Bill Jesse (*Riff-Raff*).

I remember once presiding over the International Critics' Jury at Cannes and, as the British representative, gingerly suggesting that one of Loach's films should at least be on the short-list. 'What?' said several members of the jury in unison, 'On the short-list? He's got to win!' One of them, a Latin American, added: 'Who else can make you laugh and then cry in the space of two minutes?' He's a director admired, and often loved, all over the world.

YOUNG MR LINCOLN

Directed by John Ford
With Henry Fonda, Alice Brady, Pauline Moore, Ward Bond
USA, 1939, 101 minutes

'It's no use asking me to talk about art' – John Ford. 'Oh, yes. He was a great bullshitter' – Henry Fonda.

Clearly John Ford would not have been at home doing two days of group interviews about his latest film at Cannes. Nor was he much at home doing interviews of any sort, especially with critics. He once accorded me a session at Venice, bawling out from the lavatory by way of introduction: 'Come on in – I can deal with two shits at once'. As Lindsay Anderson once wrote: 'I more or less reconciled myself that admiration was better from afar'.

But whatever he said, artist he was, and a great cinematic poet too, working at a time when his fond investigation of the American past had to connect with both the considerable constraints of Hollywood and the immediate hopes and fears of American society.

It would be completely wrong to think that he was working in isolation from his times. Almost all his films were edited by others, which is why he always tried to shoot a minimum of footage to give his cutter as little opportunity as possible.

A number of his films would easily qualify for inclusion among the best – three from 1939 alone in *Stagecoach*, the first film he shot with John Wayne in Monument Valley (which afterwards came to be known as Ford country), *Young Mr Lincoln*, his first with Henry Fonda, and *Drums Along the Mohawk*.

Fonda, like Wayne, was central to Ford's art, but whereas Wayne was the perfect expression of Ford's love of tradition and an often nostalgic and idealised past, Fonda lent his films the idea that there could be an optimistic future too.

Young Mr Lincoln was about the early life of Abraham Lincoln, his love for Ann Rutledge, which ended tragically, his decision to become a lawyer, and his first trial, in which he successfully defended two brothers on a murder charge.

The film is based upon the fact that everyone who watched it knew who Lincoln was, and was designed to show that even as a young man there was greatness in him. In France, it was rather literally called *Towards His Destiny*.

A simple plan, perhaps, and not without a measure of sentimental pieties. But this is still a deeply moving film, with certain sequences that express all, or at least most, of Ford's basic, and often contradictory, philosophy.

One of them is when Lincoln first visits Ann's grave in late winter as the ice breaks up on the river. Talking to her about his future, he decides to hold up a stick and let it drop. If it falls towards him, he will stay where he is in the country. If it falls away from him towards Ann's body, he will go to town and practise law. It falls towards her. But we are allowed to guess that he helped it along anyway.

The scene, gentle and done with great economy, so that it doesn't seem hopelessly simplistic, expresses a lot about Ford – it was his way of saying that to honour the dead properly you have to fulfil the aspirations they had for you.

Time and again the film is organised around such crucial Fordian values. But it very seldom seems self-conscious. The wider resonances are effectively underlined by film-making that never takes its eyes off the story it is telling.

Fonda's performance was once considered the sole reason for the film's success, and it is extraordinarily subtle even as it looks direct and simple. But *Young Mr Lincoln's* craftsmanship is what looks classic now, as does the potent quality of its myth-making, mixing with flawless skill the comedy of the pie-judging and tug-of-war contests in small-town America and the tension of Lincoln's speech from the prison steps to the Springfield lynch mob.

'I may not know much about the law,' says Lincoln at the murder trial, 'But I know what is right!' Thus the former store-keeper and hick lawyer becomes a man of destiny – another typical Fordian concept, encapsulating the idea that there is a higher law that civilisation neglects at its peril, and it has to do with family and community, and a shared struggle for survival.

THE STRIKE

Directed by Sergei Eisenstein
With Grigori Alexandrov, Maxim Strauch
USSR, 1924, 96 minutes

Brilliant and original film-maker and theorist as Sergei Eisenstein was, his influence was never quite as great as some once supposed. Nor has his critical reputation survived the passing of the years totally intact. Yet, as Ronald Bergan points out in his new study, *Eisenstein: A Life In Conflict*, he was much more than the 'cold-blooded montage maniac' of the Russian Revolution, who regarded 'the people' as more important than individuals.

He was an intensely cultivated man who preferred art and philosophy to political theory, adored the best of Disney and Chaplin as much as he hated the worst of Stalin, and was not above sketching semi-pornographic drawings in his spare time. A complicated man, in fact. But the fact that Bergan feels it necessary to defend him tells its own story.

The films do lack a certain humanity. *Battleship Potemkin* and *October* were two masterpieces of film technique, to which contemporary film-makers still bow today (witness the shot-for-shot homage to the Odessa Steps sequence in Brian De Palma's *The Untouchables* and Jean-Luc Godard's tribute to him in *Les Carabiniers*). *Alexander Nevsky* and the two parts of *Ivan The Terrible* were operatic and often grotesque, but classics too. Only *Strike*, his first feature, made at the early age of twenty-six, show his basic humanity, and it is arguably his best because of it.

The film, which some people persist in thinking was but a rough sketch for *Potemkin*, but which has the freshness and audacity of something more than that, is the story of a strike by factory workers in the Tsarist Russia of 1912 and its brutal suppression. It was supposed to be the first of a series of films on the development of the workers' struggle, but was the only one actually to be made.

It was shot almost entirely on location so that it seemed like a recon-struction of actual events, though its theatrical origins are obvious and its caricatures of the factory bosses are hardly realist – especially when dwarfs do a tango for them on a table groaning under caviar and campagne. But, though it was about 'the workers' rather than individuals, and opens with a worthy quote from Lenin, several characters stand out, like the two young leaders of the strike and the worker who hangs himself when falsely accused of theft.

The whole film is as angry as any Eisenstein made – 'I don't make films to be watched by an impassive eye,' he once said. 'I prefer to hit people hard on the nose.' It doesn't always work. The intercutting of the final massacre at the factory with shots of the slaughter of cattle at an abattoir now seems far too blatant.

But sequence after sequence does hit us pretty hard on the nose, including another piece of cross-cutting between the police moving into action against the strikers and one of the factory owners casually mani-pulating a lemon-squeezer. Time and again the film achieves an emotional level that, apart from some of the extant sequences of *Que Viva Mexico!*, can't be found so strongly in the rest of his work.

Eisenstein remains an extraordinary figure in the history of the cinema because of his passionate conviction in the justice of the Russian Revolution and because of the techniques he developed to propagandise it on film. That this was wonderfully exciting cinema is beyond question, and it left its mark. But, despite all the homages to him, the cinema has by and large gone in a different direction.

As Bergan says in his final chapter: 'Eisenstein, in his writings and films, led the storming of the palaces of bourgeois culture, only to find himself continually trampled underfoot in the manner of his beloved Charlie the tramp'. But he always retained both his irreverent sense of humour and his dream of creating 'an unheard-of form of cinema which inculcates the Revolution into the general history of culture, creating a synthesis of science, art and militant class consciousness'.

BOUDU SAVED FROM DROWNING

Directed by Jean Renoir
With Michel Simon, Charles Granval
France, 1932, 83 minutes

'Everyone has his reasons,' Jean Renoir used to say, and his generosity of spirit is what elevates his films so high in the estimation of successive generations of film-goers. Just occasionally, however, one has to ask whether Hitler had his reasons too. 'If every way of life can be defended,' the critic Robin Wood has commented, 'then nothing need be changed'.

Renoir, however, did not become the father-figure of the French New Wave for his human warmth and moderation. And it was *Boudu Saved From Drowning* rather than the more famous *La Grande Illusion* and *Rules of the Game*, great classics as they are, that convinced the young New Wave bloods that here was a precursor who deserved to be followed.

Boudu (Michel Simon) is a terminally scruffy tramp who is saved from drowning in the Seine by an antiquarian bookseller (Charles Granval). Apparently, the man was fed up with life and intending suicide. And now he insists that his rescuer must take responsibility for him. Brought back to the bookseller's bougeois household, he behaves exactly as nature rather than propriety demands.

The family are shocked but patronisingly amused at first, even when Boudu spits on the beloved editions of Balzac belonging to the antiquarian. He does so not out of spite but simply because you spit when you want to spit. But when Boudu, responding to what is clearly a rather different call of nature to that meant by the phrase now, seduces first the wife and then the maid, we begin to understand that the two worlds of the middle class and the outsider are colliding with fatal results.

Eventually the tramp, who had apparently never kissed anybody before except his dog, marries the pretty maid but, accidentally this time and probably the worse for drink, falls in the river after the ceremony. Suddenly discovering his liberty again, he's off to pastures new.

The film is actually based on a play in which Boudu finally accepts his responsibilities. But Renoir wanted a joyful paean to freedom and anarchy, to be contrasted with the plodding pursuit of material comforts the bookseller's family was engaged in. And so the film looks even more appropriate now than it ever did, right down to the military bugle sounding as Boudu beds the bookseller's wife.

What the New Wavers liked, apart from the subversive nature of the material, and what may seem to us old hat by now, is the fact that everything was shot on location – Paris and its quays, the bookseller's stuffy household, and the then-beautiful suburban countryside are summoned up with great eloquence and skill. And if Renoir seems to like everybody, especially Boudu, can one really cavil?

Simon, given as much freedom as possible by his director, manages to seem charming even when behaving like a complete slob. And here a few doubts surface in this delicious film. For instance, how threatening is Boudu in reality? And should we be laughing when he virtually rapes the bookseller's wife? The scene is played as farce and so works all right. But could it be played as such now?

Renoir, however, was a master who seemed incapable of making a bad film, but modest enough to admit his own flaws. His total lack of cynicism or even pessimism is what attracts people to his films today. That and the kind of fluency of utterance that makes you totally unaware of his film-making technique, which always manages to show you not only what goes on within the frame but also to suggest the world beyond it.

He is generally considered one of the very greatest film-makers of all time, largely because he could so clearly convey his humanity and warmth through his films. But he wasn't simply loveable. Like his painter father, he expressed far more than at first meets the eye.

SHOCK CORRIDOR

Directed by Sam Fuller
With Peter Breck, Constance Towers, Gene Evans
USA, 1963, 101 minutes

'*Shock Corridor* is not only outright trash, but stands also as one of the most vicious and irresponsible pieces of film-making that the screen has given us in years.'
This kind of American review, which characterised Sam Fuller as a right-wing vulgarian – a yellow journalist transforming himself into a purple film-maker – was once so prevalent that when the French started fashioning him into an *auteur* on the same level as Nicholas Ray, or even Hawks and Ford, absurdity seemed to be being piled upon absurdity.

That Fuller was a remarkable film-maker there is no doubt. But that doesn't mean we have to accept every film he made as some kind of gospel. You certainly can't accept *Shock Corridor* as such. But I defy anyone to see it for the first time and not be in some way amazed, perhaps by its energy or certainly by its passionate crudity.

Johnny, the central character, is a crime reporter, like Fuller once was. A man called Sloane has been murdered in a mental hospital, and he persuades his editor that he should be passed off as insane in order to get inside the asylum, solve the case and thus qualify for the Pulitzer Prize.

Cathy, his stripper girlfriend – characterised in the screenplay thus: 'Her body is a symphony, her legs a rhapsody', and later told that her mouth is a tunnel – is reluctantly forced to say that she's his sister and he's been making incestuous advances. After questioning he's admitted for sexual therapy.

But faced by the inmates, one of whom was once a genius who helped to create the atom bomb and who may or may not have witnessed the murder, Johnny's own mind begins to snap. Attacked by voracious patients in the nympho ward, he starts to believe Cathy really is his sister, and he's given shock treatment. In the end he finds the killer, and looks like getting his Pulitzer Prize, but is too insane even to feel Cathy's desperate hug.

Such a story, if put before your average producer now, would undoubtedly be laughed out of court. It's trashy, lurid, preposterous. But you can't take your eyes off the screen because, despite the tatty sets and often ludicrous lines, the film-making is incredibly brave, direct and furious. The whole thing is like a thunderstorm.

What does it say? Not a lot about mental asylums, awful as they probably were at the time. But quite a lot about America when you consider

the patients. One of them let down his country as a soldier in Korea and was branded a traitor, another couldn't stand the pressures of being a black guinea-pig at an all-white Southern college, a third realised what he had done working on the Bomb.

As for Johnny, he is obsessed not with justice but with his own ambition. The only truly sympathetic character in the movie is Cathy, the desired but looked-down-upon stripper. If her mouth is a tunnel, it's the only one that speaks consistent sense.

Possibly Fuller made better films, like *The Naked Kiss* and *Pick Up on South Street*. *Shock Corridor*, though, is a pretty good introduction to the artless art of a true original.

I did two *Guardian* interviews with him as an old and still incredibly energetic man. But by that time he had cast himself, chewing his regulation cigar and spitting out aphorisms, in the guise expected of him by his adoring fans and, vastly entertaining as it was, you couldn't get beyond that to the real man.

Truffaut, however, put his worth as well as any. 'Sam Fuller,' he wrote, 'is not a beginner, he is a primitive; his mind is not rudimentary, it is rude; his films are not simplistic, they are simple, and it is this simplicity I most admire'.

ANTONIO DAS MORTES

Directed by Glauber Rocha
With Mauricio Do Valle, Odete Lara
Brazil, 1969, 95 minutes

At the top of the certificates handed out at film festivals to the winners of the International Critics' Awards is a simple drawing by Glauber Rocha, the leading light of the Brazilian Cinema Novo which revolutionised cinema in that country in the sixties and became admired throughout the world. At one point, an all-night screening of Cinema Novo films at the National Film Theatre in London was hopelessly over-subscribed.

But the movement, encouraged by the period of democracy instigated by the fall of the dictator Getulio Vargas and the emergence of the liberal President Goulart, was stunted by the return of the generals, for whom the outpouring of dozens of radical films proved a threat they could not countenance. Rocha, potentially a great film-maker, died a disappointed and drug and alcohol-riven man at the age of only forty-three in 1981.

The fact is, though, that Cinema Novo, which presented itself as a political and popular cinema, never built an effective bridge between the Latin American bourgeoisie and the masses it was supposed to emancipate. Glauber Rocha's films, however, remain an extraordinary legacy of the greatest days of the Brazilian cinema.

His first feature was *Barravento* (*The Turning Wind*) in which a radical from the city attempts to stir up the fishermen of the remote coastal region of Bahia. Good as it was, there were few hints in it of the epic *Black God, White Devil* which followed.

The film takes place on the *sertao*, the bleak and parched lands of northern Brazil, where a poverty-stricken cowpoke kills his abusive boss, and becomes an outlaw and the disciple of a black religious revolutionary who preaches that violence is the only way out. Folk songs and the music of Villa Lobos and even Bach illustrate the symbolic story, the style of which seems like that of Italian neo-realism infected by the cutting of Eisenstein and the audacity of the French New Wave.

If this hit Western viewers like a rebellious clap of thunder in 1964, *Antonio Das Mortes*, made five years later in the same spectacular territory, confirmed the director's stature by winning him the Best Director Award at Cannes. In it, a hired killer (almost a Brazilian version of a samurai), after mercilessly tracking down and killing insurgents, decides to side with the peasants agains the brutal and unfeeling landlords.

The whole film is much like an epic and polemical poem, lionising revolutionaries like Che Guevara as it lovingly photographs the mountains and plains of the country – a land whose people are being destroyed by post-colonial exploitation. Rocha originally called the film *The Dragon of Evil Against the Warrior Saint*, with the landlord Horacio as the dragon, accompanied by the attractive and enigmatic Laura, one of several female figures Rocha seemed to regard as very capable of treachery.

The film is not, however, at all straightforward in its political thrust in other directions as well, since the semi-pagan religion and *macumba* trance dancing that always fascinated the director is seen as capable of aligning with the Catholic Church on the side of revolution. There is also a drunken and disillusioned middle-class school teacher (shades of Hawks's *Rio Bravo*) who pulls himself together to fight side-by-side with Antonio.

The film is as violent as any made in Latin America – 'Only when he is confronted with violence can the coloniser understand, through horror, the strength of the culture he exploits'. But it is largely ritualised and theatrical, such as when Antonio and the bandit Coirana circle round each other, each clenching one end of the same pink scarf between his teeth.

Antonio das Mortes is a unique film of great beauty and power in which music and images gel together to produce something much more than a tract. If Rocha eventually realised that art was incapable of producing change, at least he made a notable attempt to see if it could.

LOVE

Directed by Károly Makk
With Lili Darvas, Mari Torocsik, Ivan Darvas
Hungary, 1971, 92 minutes

Directors fighting against seemingly insuperable odds often make their finest films. That was frequently true of the film-makers of what was once called Eastern Europe, where the authorities took pride in supporting film far more than those of the capitalist West, but where there was also constant political censorship.

'It's dangerous,' the great Polish director Andrzej Wajda once said to me, 'but there are ways to get round political censorship, which is often pretty dumb. There are, however, no ways to get round the censorship of money you have in the West, which is even dumber but much stronger.'

It was managed in Hungary as often as anywhere else, and in Károly Makk's *Love* with particular success. Makk was a director who invariably took risks but had to wait five or six years before he could make *Love*, one of the most moving commentaries on what it is like to live under political tyranny I've ever seen.

The tyrant concerned was Rakosi, one of the last of the Russian puppets who ruled Hungary with a rod of iron, causing political opponents to disappear, often never to be seen again. One such prisoner is Janos, in jail on a trumped-up charge. His wife and a sick old mother await his return home.

His wife, in order to sustain the old lady, tells her that her son is pursuing a successful career as a Hollywood director, and reads her letters purporting to come from America. She herself is in trouble since she has lost her job and thus her livelihood because of her political connections. We never quite know whether the old lady believes her or not, nor whether her own tales about a glamorous childhood in Vienna are fantasy.

Finally, the prison doors open and the man is freed. He travels home almost in dread of what, after all these years, he might find there.

Makk's haunting, atmospheric and beautifully performed film, brilliantly shot by Janos Toth, captures exactly the fear and uncertainty of the time. It is, above all, a treatise on how such times affect any concept of fidelity, faith, illusion and even love. Taken from stories by Tibor Dery, it deals specifically with Hungary but has an absolutely universal appeal.

The role of the mother is played by the writer Ferenc Molnar's widow, Lily Darvas, who had lived in the States since the thirties but returned to Hungary for this film. She is superb, and rightly won great praise when the film was shown abroad just before she died. But Mari Torocsik, one of Hungary's best young actresses, is also totally believable as the wife, as is Ivan Darvas as the sick and greying prisoner.

The film is tough as old boots and completely unsentimental, but its camera catches precisely what its three leading characters face and how they feel. It is sometimes quite difficult to bear because of the nature of the truths it tells. The prisoner's journey home, for instance, is a sequence during which Makk and his actor express everything necessary to make us understand not just the joy of freedom but the fear of finding that those he loves have either forgotten or somehow freed themselves from him.

Makk did not make such an outstanding film again, though he was never other than a capable director. Perhaps it is true sometimes that a film-maker has one classic in him and no more, and everything he wishes to say is said there almost perfectly and in a way that it is impossible to repeat.

PATHS OF GLORY

Directed by Stanley Kubrick
With Kirk Douglas, Adolphe Menjou, Ralph Meeker
USA, 1957, 86 minutes

When a director of the stature of Stanley Kubrick dies unexpectedly, we are all forced, even if critical of some of his work, to recognise how much the cinema owes to him. He made films throughout a time when it was still possible, if difficult, for the best men and women in Hollywood to make seriously intelligent films, and when that era virtually ceased he had enough clout to buck the trend and still work without interference.

In this he was almost unique – more fortunate than Orson Welles, for instance. One only wonders whether a new Kubrick, if we were lucky enough to find one, would be so fortunate starting work today.

One of his early films is *Paths Of Glory*, a classic about individuals at war which is much more than the equal of Spielberg's *Saving Private Ryan* or Terrence Malick's *The Thin Red Line*. It is nothing like as well known to the general public as *A Clockwork Orange*, *Dr Strangelove*, *2001*, *A Space Odyssey* or *The Shining*. But it is arguably one of his very finest films.

This may have been because he made it (in 1957) when what he wanted to say emotionally was less clouded by his later, colder fascination with the logistics of film-making. Also, the essential pessimism of his later work had not yet surfaced.

The story has a classic simplicity about it that renders its argument as powerful now as it was then. Set during the First World War, it has a French general given impossible orders by his superiors to capture a well-defended enemy fortification. He passes them on to a subordinate, who passes the buck again. Each knows the impossibility of the task, and when it fails the third officer (Colonel Dax, played by Kirk Douglas) is the logical choice to take responsibility, and he wishes to do so. His superiors, however, refuse to let him.

Three representatives of the men, chosen by each company commander, must be sacrificed instead, and Colonel Dax nobly if guiltily takes on the hopeless task of defending them against a charge of cowardice. The paths of glory do indeed lead but to the grave.

Kubrick's film is clearly an angry one – he was basically an old-fashioned Jewish liberal brought up in the Bronx. But *Paths of Glory* is as much concerned to tell us about the pattern of human behaviour as to be a piece of anti-establishment propaganda.

The General, superbly played by Adolphe Menjou, shows no emotion at all in insisting that the men rather than the officers take the blame. He

does what he is supposed to do according to his station in life. In a way, Colonel Dax is the weaker man, betrayed by his emotions but unable to contemplate what Spartacus (also played by Douglas in the later film) did by engineering a revolt against injustice. Nor are the men much better. They also haven't the strength of will to contest their lot. Nor a leader to help them.

Humphrey Cobb's book, from which the story is culled, is more simplistic than this – it tells you what to think. Kubrick's film knows what you may think, but never anticipates it. It divides the world into two different places. The mud-grey world of the trenches is one, the rococo chateau where the officers live is another.

'There is no such thing as shell-shock,' says the General, inspecting his troops and coming across a trembling man, 'Get him out of here. I won't have brave men contaminated.'

Kubrick was aided by black-and-white photography from George Krause which was brilliantly modelled on the work of front-line photographers of the time and by a sound-track much subtler than that available to Lewis Milestone in the earlier classic *All Quiet On The Western Front*.

There is, for instance, a deafening silence before the unfortunate soldiers are shot in the early morning light, and the shots themselves seem to wake the birds. What we have here is a masterly sense of atmosphere which tells us everything, and more, of what Kubrick wants us to know.

This is a film which, though largely populated by American actors, seems more European than most European films. It isn't too fanciful to say that the later *Dr Strangelove*, which mined the same general theme and turned it into farce, was a logical extension of *Paths of Glory*.

In almost every film he made, it was the frailties of human beings faced with an often ridiculous and dangerously exploitative system that were Kubrick's main concern. *Paths of Glory* is possibly his most emotional film, and that's why I think it remains one of his best.

KINGS OF THE ROAD

Directed and written by Wim Wenders
With Rudiger Vogler, Hanns Zischler
Germany, 1976, 176 minutes

There was a time when Wim Wenders, the German film-maker, was second only to Rainer Werner Fassbinder as a god of the New German Cinema – a poet of the screen who both idolised the American cinema, like the practitioners of the earlier French New Wave, and was repelled and frustrated by the dominance of Hollywood. This ambivalence proved his undoing, since only his closest supporters could see how he intended to improve on the basic story-telling tenets of the American cinema, or how his kind of European art movie could possibly challenge Hollywood.

But if he is now a figure in decline, at least four of his films can be considered as good as anything else being made at what was a pretty good time. They were, in my estimation, *Alice in the Cities*, *The State of Things*, *Kings of the Road* and *Paris, Texas*. The last was the only really good film he made in America, and Ry Cooder's music plus Harry Dean Stanton's persona were as much responsible as the director for that. My choice, however, is *Kings of the Road*.

Its two unsettled travellers wandering along the backroads of provincial West Germany near the border with the East are a repairer of film projection equipment (Rudy Vogler, one of Wenders' favourite actors) and a linguist (Hanns Zischler) who tags along with him after a half-hearted suicide attempt. They are typical representatives of the Germany of the time, uncertain about their place in the scheme of things, worried about the future. And what they find en route is dilapidated and virtually deserted cinemas, except for those showing Hollywood films. The great heritage of the pre-Nazi German cinema seems dead and gone.

The film has only the most fractured of narratives and a very spare script as the pair eat, drink, meet people and wander the route chosen by the repairman. But the German title *Im Lauf Der Zeit* (*In the Course of Time*) gives us a clue as to why we are so affected by it. It builds steadily in the mind as a quiet study of the walls not only between East and West Germany, and between imported American culture and European sensibilities, but between ordinary people too.

There's not much moralising or philosophy behind *Kings of the Road*, and certainly none of the slightly portentous complications with which Wenders has afflicted us of late (*Million Dollar Hotel*, for instance). What he achieves instead is a palpable sense of time, place and atmosphere, and of how everybody is affected by their tiny spot in the history of their countries.

What could have been a dull work, considering its almost three-hour length and lack of drama, looks as good today as it ever did. Despite being tied irrevocably to the seventies, it carries an appeal for film students second to none. Robby Muller, one of the world's most eloquent cinematophers, contributes mightily to this, since its images are so perfect, and so does Wenders's choice of the music of the time, often American. There is an almost hypnotic quality about the film – Europe's most telling example of the American road movie.

Some directors, like Buñuel, Hawks, Ford and Bergman can spend a lifetime making good movies. But perhaps because Wenders came to the fore in a very specific time – his first feature was made in 1970 – he has seemed unable to progress, at least into the nineties and the new century.

You feel that if Fassbinder had not destroyed himself he would have had as much to say now as at the time of his prime. Possibly hampered by the gaggle of starry-eyed supporters who invariably surround him, Wenders is walking the same path while most of his audience has some time ago decided on another one.

THE TREE OF THE WOODEN CLOGS

Directed by Ermanno Olmi
With the people of Bergamo
Italy, 1978, 180 minutes

No other Italian film-maker of world stature has been as neglected as Ermanno Olmi, possibly because his quiet mastery is unfashionable now but substantially because a serious illness has limited his capacities in recent years. The last time he came into prominence was in 1978, when he

deservedly won the Palme d'Or at Cannes with *The Tree of the Wooden Clogs*.
Many think this three-hour epic about the lives of peasants in turn-of-the-century Bergamo is his masterwork. It may be, but other classics include *Il Posto* (*The Job*), *I Fidanzati* (*The Fiances*), *Un Certo Giorno* (*One Fine Day*) and *La Circostanza* (*The Circumstance*).

His films may not have the virtuosity of Fellini, Visconti, Pasolini and Bertolucci. But time will prove they are of equal value and longevity.

The Tree of the Wooden Clogs was taken from stories Olmi's grandmother told him, made with direct sound (very unusual in Italy), and used peasants from the area as actors. It was even spoken not in Italian but in Bergamesque. What it attempted was not only an attack on an outmoded social system – the peasants have to beg land and the wherewithal for a basic education from the local landlord – but an almost mystical affirmation of the relationship of man to nature.

Olmi was a Catholic as well as a Marxist, so the film is not as angry as, and is far more beautiful than, that other masterpiece of the same genre from Latin America, Nelson Periera Dos Santos's *Barren Lives*. But in some ways its sentiments are just as revolutionary as any work the Cinema Novo produced.

Its strength lies not just in its ravishing depiction of the changing seasons in a stunning part of Lombardy, nor in its human sympathies, which are never patronising to the ordinary people he finds so unordinary, but in its measured, cumulative approach to the hard life of those close to penury and exploited by the powerful. For instance, the tree of the title is the one cut down by a father to make a pair of clogs for his son to reach school. For which he pays a terrible price.

There are several other stunning sequences, such as when a secretive old man finally tells his grand-daughter how he has managed to grow his tomato crop early each year so that he can be the first to sell in the market. Even better is the honeymoon trip on an old barge of two wide-eyed young lovers to the big city of Milan.

In a way this is a documentary that isn't a documentary, perhaps a trifle nostalgic for times past but never averse to pointing out the viciousness of the old system and the bleak fight that has to be fought against the natural world. It has iron in its soul, but what a soul!

Olmi's other films are very different, though inhabiting the same humanist space. *Il Posto* has a young man triumphantly finding a clerking job but thereby condemned to drudgery for the rest of his life. *One Fine Day* has a middle-aged businessman causing an accident in which a farm-worker dies and being forced to re-examine his whole empty life because of it.

'Work,' Olmi once said, 'is not a damnation for man. It is his chance to express himself. But work as it is organised by society often becomes a condemnation. It annuls man.' He added: 'We are conditioned, but we are also guilty of letting it happen'.

His precise and tactful films never rail, never ask you to weep, and never over-dramatise. They simply seem to exist naturally, setting the characters against an equally authentic background so that you forget the skill with which they are certainly made.

It is good to know that many of the better present-day Italian film-makers regard his work as a model. So far, however, they have not emulated it.

BEHIND THE GREEN DOOR

Directed by Jim and Art Mitchell
With Marilyn Chambers, Johnny Keyes
USA, 1972, 72 minutes

Pornography has been with us a great deal longer than the cinema. But it's certainly been a staple of the cinema from the year dot. At no time, how-ever, was it so acceptable as in the America of the early seventies. Hardcore porn was shown at that time in perfectly respectable mainstream cinemas, and perfectly respectable couples, even their college-educated kids, would not care a jot if anyone saw them going in or coming out.

Now such films, or the much more sleazy and slap-dash modern equivalents, are relegated either to backstreet porno houses or to the pay-TV channels you can get in hotel rooms (other than in Dirty Mac Britain, where soft porn like *Danish Dentist on the Job* is the most you can expect). Have we progressed or declined in this matter? It isn't my job to find an answer to that question. But I can say that there were breakthrough porn movies which deserved at least some of the limelight they were once afforded.

The two directors who were certainly pioneers were Gerard Damiano (*Deep Throat* and *The Devil in Miss Jones*) and the Mitchell Brothers, who made one of the most successful of them all – *Behind the Green Door*. This was the most stylish, and some say the most erotic, of all of them. But then eroticism is in the eye of the beholder and can't very successfully be measured by a critic.

I remember giving a good review to a decidedly saucy film being shown in the depths of Soho, and being told by a leader writer at the *Guardian*, who went, that he was embarassed to find 'several bishops and half the Houses of Parliament' in the queue outside. And admittedly part of the success of *Behind the Green Door*, always slaughtered by the Censor in this country, was the fact that Marilyn Chambers, its star, pleasured by nuns, a well-known boxer and three trapeze artists in the film, was also the '99.44 per cent pure Ivory Snow Girl' of advertising fame at the time.

She became an instant celebrity, was invited onto talk shows, and behaved like the Hollywood star she might have been in different circumstances. Serious critics reviewed the film – and were not all that snooty about it – while it raced up the list of the most popular movies as if nothing untoward was happening at all.

It was Damiano's *Deep Throat*, a rather messy endeavour to say the least, concentrating on fellatio, that made porn fashionable in the first place, with Linda Lovelace becoming a chic household name. But while Damiano strived for raunchy impact, and urged his women on to ever-more-extreme sexual gymnastics, the Mitchell Brothers opted for 'art' and a semblance of respectability, and were delighted that it was women rather than men who were the bedrock of their audience.

Because of this, there were as many female commentators who approved of the film as disapproved, since it was about a woman totally liberated by experiences which had previously been part of her private and unattainable fantasies.

I have to say that the climax of the film, which lasts for several minutes and has one of the trapeze artists ejaculating into the heroine's mouth in extreme slow motion, reworked over and over again by means of dissolves and other special effects, now seems more hilarious than arty. But the film does have a charge to it you can't deny, Chambers is certainly some sort of an actress as well as being beautiful, and the Mitchell Brothers could at least claim some imagination in making it.

As for Chambers, she was well paid for her pains and received a cut of the film's profits that made her rich as well as famous. If she was exploited, there were considerable compensations.

PANDORA'S BOX

Directed by G.W. Pabst
With Louise Brooks, Fritz Kortner, Franz Lederer, Alice Roberts,
Gustav Diessl
Germany, 1929, 131 minutes

Critical fashions come and go, and for some time Fritz Lang and F.W. Murnau were up and G.W. Pabst was down where German film-makers of the twenties and early thirties are concerned. Pabst is now being recognised again as a remarkable director, capable of creating films in which atmosphere is as much created by small detail as by more grandiose effects.

He was also an actor's director, and his most memorable star was Louise Brooks, the American actress who found in him the perfect foil for her talents in *Pandora's Box* (alternatively titled *Lulu*) and *Diary of a Lost Girl*. She was the Marilyn Monroe of her time, of whom a French critic wrote: 'She is the only woman who has the ability to transfigure no matter what film into a masterpiece'.

After these two films for Pabst, this ex-Ziegfeld Follies girl known for liking a good time but also for reading Schopenhauer between takes, went back to America and began a tragic slide into destitution.

She was rediscovered in the fifties when Kenneth Tynan wrote a remarkable essay about her and Henri Langlois, the famous head of the French Cinématheque, uttered the memorable words: 'There is no Garbo. There is no Dietrich. There is only Louise Brooks!'

Much more intelligent than the parts she had to play in Hollywood, Brooks found in Wedekind's *Lulu*, renamed *Pandora's Box* by Pabst, the perfect expression of her beauty and eroticism. Many think the part chased her for the rest of her life. In fact, once rediscovered, she became a writer and critic of some note before she died in 1985.

Pabst made sure that Brooks was pre-eminently Wedekind's idea of *Lulu* – a beautiful innocent who passively accepts her sexuality and causes the weak men who adore her to self-destruct. She is the prostitute

as scapegoat, tragic but with no sense of sin, who is eventually killed by
Jack the Ripper.

Pabst realised that, as well as being a beautiful woman, Brooks was an
actress who, since she was once a dancer, could move across the screen in
a way which expressed feelings much as others do with their faces. He
gave her dresses which symbolised her character and condition – spotless

white satin when she kills her husband, and dirty garments when she picks up the Ripper on the foggy London street.

Those who think the merits of the film are entirely those of Brooks take no account of this or the way Pabst created the atmosphere of sexual delirium that prevades what was at that time a dangerously shocking film. It still remains an intensely sexy one. This was also expressionism put to use with unerring skill as a commentary on the social hypocrisy of the time.

Pabst was condemned in Germany for making a scandalous version of the play which hitherto had been performed as if Lulu was a man-eater devouring her sexual victims (Asta Nielsen in the film *Loulou*). There was also the shock of the cinema's first openly lesbian scene, in which the Belgian actress Alice Roberts, as Countess Geschwitz, attempts to make love to Lulu.

Brooks herself was castigated at the time as a non-actress (perhaps because she was not German). And even during the shooting there was controversy, with Kortner, the famous German actor who played Dr Schon – who would have doubtless preferred the young and then rather tarty-looking Marlene Dietrich in the part – refusing to speak to Brooks throughout.

In Britain, the lesbian episodes were excised, and in France Lulu's death at the hands of the Ripper was substituted for her conversion by the Salvation Army. Both *Pandora's Box* and *Diary of a Lost Girl* were soon stored away and the original uncut versions misplaced. But in the fifties these two extraordinary works, illuminating the power and presence of a great star, came to be put beside *Joyless Street*, *The Threepenny Opera*, *Westfront* and *Kameradschaft* as Pabst's masterworks.

THE BITTER TEA OF GENERAL YEN

Directed by Frank Capra
With Barbara Stanwyck, Nils Asther
USA, 1933, 87 minutes

'Buddha, Joan of Arc and the spirit of all who believe in God live in the White House,' Spencer Tracy was made to say in *State of the Union*, a dreadful film made by Frank Capra in 1948. It was the logical conclusion to this Sicilian immigrant's admiration for America – a doting which admittedly produced much better movies, like *It Happened One Night* and *Mr Deeds Goes To Town*.

But even these affectionately remembered films look naive and sentimental now, despite the very evident skill of their making. The former won Capra the Oscars he craved. He called them 'my holy grail'. Shrewd and talented as he was, Capra's espousals of the virtues of the little man reek of whimsy and wishful thinking and, though we were once taken in by their sheer entertertainment value, remain among the American cinema's most cosily absurd fables.

Not long after he made *State Of The Union*, this somewhat unpleasing man was convinced that the America he once loved, and who had once loved his work, had been taken over by gays, druggies and draft-dodgers. Unfortunately he funked making a movie about that. But, much earlier in his pretty long career, he did make one extraordinary film. It was called *The Bitter Tea of General Yen*, an exotic fable that showed him capable of what producer Harry Cohn called 'the sort of arty junk that wins Oscars'.

It was neither arty nor junk, but a very skillful adaptation of a novel about a prim New England girl (Barbara Stanwyck) who arrives in Shanghai to marry a tight-arsed missionary as civil war breaks out. Attempting to save some children, she gets knocked flat and awakes in the train of a notorious Chinese warlord (Nils Asther). Taken to his summer palace, and held by the fascinated infidel, she starts to try to convert him. But she also begins to dress in Chinese gowns and to fall in love with a surprisingly wise and courtly man. Alas, however, the war turns against him and he poisons himself.

It's a tale made both credible and erotic by Joe Walker, Capra's cameraman, screenwriter Edward Paramore and Stanwyck, an actress it was always difficult to look away from (here she has seldom seemed so innocently beautiful). And we have to credit Capra too for seeing in it a kind of Jamesian intelligence, and playing that up together with the sexual connotations.

The film looks marvellous, almost in the Sternberg mould, with black-and-white lighting culled from special portrait lenses and the sort of richly textured decor that only MGM could contemplate at the time. The dream sequence is particularly striking. The American girl sees a couple courting before retiring to bed. Her bedroom door is broken open by a threatening Chinaman, but she is saved by a masked man in Western clothes. When he takes his mask off, it is General Yen. They sink back onto the bed, and as she wakes from her dream she finds the General standing above her prone figure.

It was only later that Capra began his patriotic Americana. Before that, he seemed capable of superbly crafted movies – an eclectic talent who turned into a careerist. We should perhaps not mock films like *It Happened One Night*. They were made in an era when Capra wasn't the only one fooled by the American dream. But we should certainly regret that such a good film-maker got down to thinking that Buddha was likely to be comfortable in the White House.

THE ROUND-UP

Directed by Miklós Jancsó
With Janos Gorbe, Tibor Molnar
Hungary, 1965, 94 minutes

Those who have never seen a film by Miklós Jancsó when this Hungarian director was at his peak in the sixties are usually astonished by the experience. They have seen nothing like it before or since. When *The Round-up*, his third film, came to London in 1965, the broadsheet critics almost dropped their pens in surprise.

Here was a deeply serious, decidedly uncamp and certainly not musically-minded Middle European Busby Berkeley who made formal patterns with humans and horses on the screen in order to illustrate the bitter betrayals of his country's history. I joke, but not much. To watch *The Round-up* or its successor, *The Red and the White*, for the first time is to witness a kind of film ballet entering the realms of political drama.

In *The Round-up*, Austrian soldiers representing the triumphant Hapsburg Empire trap and interrogate the Hungarian partisans whose revolt against the Empire's rule has finally petered out. The period is the mid-nineteenth century, and only the legendary Sandor Rosza's fighters stand in the way, succoured by the peasants.

The drama is virtually divested of characters we can either sympathise with or hate. Instead it deals largely in formal, virtually abstract generalities. It is as if Jancsó is merely watching, regretfully conscious that there are generally those who will be killed and those whose job it is to kill them. A man running on the horizon is calmly shot down. Another is captured and taken away to be tortured. Short words of command seem to be the apotheosis of dialogue. The film achieves, in one critic's accurate view, 'a total absorption of content into form'.

All this takes place on a very particular landscape – the vast and summer-scorched Hungarian plains and grasslands, where whitewashed buildings, cloaked men and their horses seem the only occupants. It seems like a world apart, but one able to illustrate not only a specific vision of Hungarian history but part of the whole story of mankind, in which the powerful slowly but surely triumph over the weak.

The film is so precisely choreographed that the patterns play on the mind until they become clear and obvious in their meanings. The camera style is beautiful but almost merciless, so that one critic's idea that it is all very like Bresson shooting Kafka seems at least partly appropriate. If the film can be criticised for its lack of emotion, it can't be for its absence of power or for its cold appreciation of the situation it illustrates.

Later, with films like *The Confrontation* and *Red Psalm* – the latter composed of only 26 shots – Jancsó's work begins to lose something through familiarity, and his obsession with half-naked girls and mechanical patterns becomes enervating. And when he at length left Hungary for Italy in the seventies, making erotica like *Private Vices, Public Virtues*, based on the Mayerling story, it seemed he had little more of value to say, or no way of saying it that didn't either repeat himself or exaggerate his weaknesses.

But the first few films were astonishing, whether dealing with Kossuth's rebels of the 1860s, the Stalinist era, or the aftermath of the 1919 Hungarian revolution. They bitterly analysed the fractured history of his persecuted country, and commented too on the nature of violence in more general terms. No one has tried quite the same thing in the same way, and that is possibly his most formidable legacy.

A TOUCH OF EVIL

Directed by Orson Welles
With Orson Welles, Charlton Heston, Janet Leigh
USA, 1958, 108 minutes

It might seem a trifle eccentric to nominate Orson Welles's *A Touch of Evil* above *Citizen Kane* or *The Magnificent Ambersons* as one of my favourite 100 movies. The film, now substantially restored the way Welles wanted it, is by no means his most ambitious. But it remains a mature, complex and endlessly fascinating example of film noir, a genre that's produced more satisfying movies than most others, precisely because of its seeming lack of pretension.

The film was made in 1958, between the infinitely less satisfactory *Confidential Report* and Welles's adaptation of Kafka's *The Trial*. It was long after *Kane* and *Ambersons*, either of which should have ensured Welles a lifetime of Hollywood finance but didn't. Like them, it was generally underrated by the American critics of the time, who saw in it merely an eccentric thriller rather than a calculatedly dramatic study of the corruption of power and the difference between morality and justice.

Few seemed aware that the opening crane and tracking shot, which lasts over three minutes, would come to be regarded as one of the most extraordinary examples of Welles's technical mastery. No one, that is, except the French, who immediately proclaimed the film a masterpiece.

Welles was aided with the dark, claustrophobic look of the film by Russell Metty's mastery of noir lighting and, of course, by his own

remarkable performance as the oversized Hank Quinlan, the driven police captain who is 'a great detective but a lousy cop'.

The man is sleazy, cynical and full of hatred, but still oddly likeable. He knows that the criminals he wants to bring to justice by whatever means are that in equal measure. And there is a Shakespearean ring about his final tragedy, as if Falstaff had been transported in time.

He is merely part and parcel of a corrupt world, and somehow pathetic in that he thinks he is basically on the side of right. The Mexican he unjustly frames for murder is, we finally learn, guilty.

The story is set in a run-down border town which was actually Venice, California, where Roger Corman was later to shoot *The Wild Angels*, and populated by as unlikely a cast as Albert Zugsmith, the producer, and Universal can ever have assembled for what was intended to be a B-grade police thriller. With Welles were Charlton Heston, Janet Leigh, Joseph Cotten, Marlene Dietrich, Zsa Zsa Gabor, Akim Tamiroff, Dennis Weaver and Mercedes McCambridge.

It says a lot for Welles that he got such good performances from Heston, as the upright, rather prim narcotics investigator for the Mexican government, from Janet Leigh, as his timorous new wife who is almost raped at one point, and from Marlene Dietrich, as the prostitute Tanya, who has those famous last words on Hank: 'He was some kind of man'.

Dietrich's scenes in the brothel are made to seem as if Sternberg, the circus master of her career, was directing her again.

But if the film is noir at its best, it was made at a time when American directors, especially Welles, still looked towards Europe as much as at their own cinema, and at the German expressionism of Fritz Lang, the maker of *M*.

The film is shot through a lens which gives great depth of focus and which also deforms the perspective. It is the visual key to Quinlan's character throughout.

The moral key is quite simple, though worked out in a unique way. It is that Quinlan, betrayed by his obsession and eventually killed by his only friend, should not be able to claim, like Raskolnikov in *Crime and Punishment*, that he can 'march over corpses or wade through blood' to do what's right. Or as Heston says: 'A policeman's job is only easy in a police state. That's the whole point, captain. Who's the boss, the cop or the law?'

Plenty of films may have made this point. But *A Touch of Evil* (which Welles thought was a silly title) expresses it both more strongly and more delicately than most, because he lets us see both sides of the equation. There is a mixture of compassion and irony in all his films, and there's the feeling that the camera is also a character, watching with quizzical curiosity.

Cocteau once said of Welles that he was a giant with the face of a child. Like a child, he didn't know the meaning of fear as far as film-making was concerned, and that was substantially why his career was stunted by those who did.

A Touch of Evil could have been hopelessly melodramatic and simple-minded. It remains, however, even after repeated viewings, one of the most sophisticated, multi-faceted and watchable thrillers ever made.

LAST TANGO IN PARIS

Directed by Bernardo Bertolucci
With Marlon Brando, Maria Schneider
Italy/France, 1973, 129 minutes

From a court in Bologna which seized and banned the film: 'Obscene content offensive to public decency, characterised by an exasperating pan-sexualism for its own end, presented with obsessive self-indulgence, catering to the lowest instincts of the libido, dominated by the idea of stirring unchecked appetites for sexual pleasure, permeated by scurrilous language... accompanied offscreen by sounds, sighs and shrieks of climax pleasure'.

If this is scarcely believable, so now is Pauline Kael's *New Yorker* review: 'The movie breakthrough has finally come... This must be the most powerfully erotic movie ever made, and it may turn out to be the most liberating movie ever made, and so it's probably only natural that an audience, anticipating a voluptuous feast from the man who made *The Conformist*, and confronted with this unexpected sexuality, and the new realism it requires of the actors, should go into shock. Bertolucci and Brando have altered the face of an art form. Who was prepared for that?'

The first ban lasted only two months, though a later Italian court had a negative burned, revoked Bertolucci's civil rights for five years and gave him a four-month suspended prison sentence. In Britain, the sodomy sequence had to be cut, presumably so as not to encourage public schoolboys. Kael's 4000-word review, however, convinced most sceptics that the film was morally serious and a work of art. It is, of course. But there's such a thing as a morally serious bad work of art too.

It is certainly the film which catapulted Bertolucci towards international fame – the story of a middle-aged man who, devastated by the apparent suicide of his wife, embarks on a purely sexual sado-masochistic affair with a young girl who in the end kills him.

Throughout the film, the girl is naked and the man is not, which caused further controversy. There were two other significant reviews. One from Molly Haskell pointed out that it was women rather than men who responded to the film. 'Our rearguard fantasies of rape, sadism, submission, liberation and anonymous sex are as important a key to our emacipation, our self-understanding, as our more advanced and admirable efforts at self-definition'. Then there was Norman Mailer, who said that the real thrill of the film was the peep-hole an improvising Brando offered us on Brando.

Maria Schneider, the girl, was unknown at the time and Bertolucci, who failed to cast both Dominique Sanda and Catherine Deneuve when both became pregnant, has said that he wanted her to be a Lolita but more perverse. He chose Brando after seeing a Francis Bacon painting 'of a man in great despair who had the air of total disillusionment'. Certainly it is a performance of extraordinary force, which his friend Jack Lemmon claims was based on his childhood, when he decided not to have any relationship in which he was going to 'get murdered emotionally'.

This may be the key to the film, since the pair play cruel, often childish, games with each other in between and even during their sexual bouts. She is a real child-woman – 'growing older is a crime,' she says at one point – and he is savagely escaping back into childhood. The film's imagery consistently reflects this as well as commenting on ageing and death.

Whether the film really indicts the bourgeois family structures which suppress feeling and 'civilise' the savage in us all is a moot point. But it clearly tries to do so. In the end, however, it seems too melodramatic to be entirely successful, and too much of a neat, if shocking, fantasy psychodrama to get all that near the truth.

But it does prove Brando to be a great screen actor and Bertolucci to be a director capable of the audacity of Godard and the naked power of Bergman. If *The Spider's Stratagem*, even if made for television, seems to me his best film, *Last Tango* is the one in which he takes most risks and thus causes most entirely legitimate argument.

INDEX OF FILMS

DEREK MALCOLM'S PERSONAL BEST

INDEX OF DIRECTORS

INDEX OF LEADING ACTORS